THE CUSTOMERCENTRIC SELLING®

FIELD GUIDE TO
Prospecting and Business Development

GARY WALKER

Mc
Graw
Hill
Education

New York   Chicago   San Francisco   Lisbon   London   Madrid
Mexico City   Milan   New Delhi   San Juan   Seoul
Singapore   Sydney   Toronto

1 2 3 4 5 6 7 8 9 0   QFR/QFR   1 9 8 7 6 5 4 3

ISBN   978-0-07-180805-7
MHID   0-07-180805-1

e-ISBN 978-0-07-180806-4
e-MHID   0-07-180806-X

Product or brand names used in this book may be trade names or trademarks. Where we believe that there may be proprietary claims to such trade names or trademarks, the name has been used with an initial capital or it has been capitalized in the style used by the name claimant. Regardless of the capitalization used, all such names have been used in an editorial manner without any intent to convey endorsements of or other affiliation with the name claimant. Neither the author nor the publisher intends to express any judgments as to the validity or legal status of any such proprietary claims.

McGraw-Hill books are available at special quantity discounts to use as premiums and sales promotions or for use in corporate training programs. To contact a representative, please e-mail us at bulksales@mcgraw-hill.com.

This book is printed on acid-free paper.

Contents

Acknowledgments

Writing a book is a time-consuming endeavor made even more challenging when you have a number of other things that require ongoing attention, including the subject of this book—prospecting and business development! For that reason, I'd like to thank Tim Young for helping to keep me on task throughout this project. Likewise, I'm grateful to Jill Perez, our director of marketing, who worked tirelessly to review my work, add to the content as needed, perform research, and edit and clarify my attempts at checkpoints and tests. Her efforts have helped to make this field guide a better resource for you, the reader. I am grateful to both Tim and Jill for their help.

Introduction

My partners and I have been pleasantly surprised by the success of CustomerCentric Selling® over the past decade. Tens of thousands of sales professionals have improved their selling skills by attending our workshops or by practicing the principles outlined in the first and second editions of our book *CustomerCentric Selling*, published by McGraw-Hill. Yet the enthusiastic response from readers and workshop attendees masked a need that I felt was lacking in the original CustomerCentric Selling methodology, a need that I would argue is among the most important skills a salesperson can have.

I'm referring to prospecting and business development.

That statement comes as no surprise to the thousands of salespeople who struggle to meet their sales quotas. After all, it's hard to close a sale without a prospect! Yet in this enlightened age of communication overload—with so many ways to tweet, update, text, and check in with others—how does one go about breaking into a new company to close that elusive sale?

Consider, for instance, that 92 percent of C-level executives *never* respond to e-mail blasts or cold calls. If you have been using e-mail or cold calls in an effort to win business, this fact may not come as a surprise to you. The reality is that this statistic, which comes from a paper entitled "Selling to Senior Executives," published by the Kenan-Flagler Business School at the University of North Carolina, has been rising and is likely to continue rising.

Pretty scary stuff, especially if you rely on either of these methods in an effort to generate new business from senior executives. Is it any wonder why salespeople loathe cold-call prospecting and business development? Senior executives resent the intrusion of the calls almost as much as salespeople despise making them. Being so uncomfortable on both sides of the table is no way to begin any relationship!

The frightening thing is that despite these findings, the salespeople who actually do actively prospect (those who don't just sit back and wait for marketing to provide them with a lead or for the phone to ring) continue to rely on *cold calling* and *e-mail* as their primary methods of prospecting and new business development. As a matter of fact, many companies require their salespeople to make some number of cold calls on a daily basis as one of their performance criteria. In essence then, they are being required by their employer to annoy prospective customers!

In the midst of writing this Introduction, I received an *e-mail blast* from an organization wanting to know if I would like to become a better *cold caller*. Now, knowing what I know, why would I want to improve at doing something that prospects report that they want no part of? Making my future customer displeased with me is *not* the way I want to begin a relationship.

Throughout this book and in our public workshops, I share additional insights on the effectiveness of cold calling as determined by other organizations. As for the effectiveness of e-mail, I believe that many salespeople hide behind it in an attempt to demonstrate that they are prospecting. They need to show that they are doing *something*. E-mail is safe, easy, and benign, and it does not subject the salesperson to personal rejection when the prospect simply drags it into the trash folder. However, it is not effective unless you are e-mail-blasting many thousands of faceless prospects and you are comfortable with the fact that, while your e-mail just annoyed over 90 percent of them, the few that do respond can keep your business going or help you to meet your quota.

Personally, I think there are far better ways to approach the crucial first phase of selling, prospecting, and business development, and this field guide can become your handy tool to show you how.

For just a moment, consider your own prospecting efforts. How effective have you been?

Cold calling and e-mail are what I refer to as *traditional* prospecting methods. These are the favored methods that most salespeople have been using for years. And as studies show, these methods in their current form are ineffective. One could even say that cold calling is dead. However, the use of the telephone and e-mail as tools that can be deployed by salespeople remains as relevant as ever. It is *how* we use them to engage with today's prospect and create interest that has changed and requires mastery.

In this field guide, I will share how you can use these methods and tools in new ways to improve your efficiency and the effectiveness of your prospecting and business development. Most important, you can use this guide to win more business and develop more lasting relationships with customers—relationships built on mutual trust and mutual respect that will allow you to achieve the success you want in the workplace and feel good about it. Now, let's begin!

Chapter 1

GETTING THE MOST OUT OF THIS FIELD GUIDE

Why a Field Guide?

If you are like many sales or business professionals, this is not the first business book you have had your hands on. However, it may be the first business *field guide* you have encountered.

Personally, I have gained much from reading the ideas expressed by authors in many fine professional books. Often they give me new ideas to consider as I'm relaxing on an airplane or feeling contemplative. But generally speaking, it is a one-way affair, with the role of the reader simply being to read the words neatly arranged on the pages and having to figure out how to implement the ideas the book's author suggests.

Field guides are different. They aim to strike a partnership with the reader through a collaboration of sorts, with the field guide providing facts, tips, and a frame of reference for the reader, who calls upon them at a time of need.

For example, if you are walking in the woods, you may find a field guide to mushrooms or trees a handy resource. Before you bend over and pick what you *hope* is a tasty morel mushroom, you whip out your field guide and examine the pictures and the written description carefully until you feel comfortable with your skills of identification. You are then rewarded with the most delicious mushroom you have ever savored and become something of a hero to your intrepid peers, who remain firmly entrenched in their way of doing things—and off they go to the grocery store to buy their button mushrooms.

As your knowledge grows, your confidence grows, and you move from elementary skills to more advanced techniques for identification and problem solving. As a parallel to your business objectives of prospecting for customers, perhaps you will even use a field guide to prospect for rocks, Civil War relics, or precious metals. Over time, your practiced use of field guides results in you having improved your confidence, competency, and satisfaction.

The CustomerCentric Selling Field Guide to Prospecting and Business Development is designed to help you navigate the same path in the field of prospecting for gold in the form of *new business*.

While there are words on these pages just as there are on the pages of any business book, as with all field guides the benefits accrue once you apply the tips, tools, methods, and exercises in real-world settings. This book is designed to go with you and to be practiced as much as read. There is space for you to scribble, annotate, and express your thoughts. In a way, you become a partner in finishing this book by customizing it for *you*.

Learning to Exercise

You probably are familiar with the expression "no pain, no gain." That saying permeates our culture for good reason; if you want results, you generally have to work for them. While it is not my intention to inflict pain on you, it is important for you to realize that you will need to apply yourself if you want to improve at anything. This is true for getting those ripped abs, becoming a virtuoso on the piano, or finishing that marathon. And it is even truer for becoming truly proficient at the science and art of prospecting and business development, differentiating yourself from the masses of salespeople.

Funny thing, though, about the profession of selling; there are far too many people who act as if you can walk right into success with no planning, no forethought, and no practice. More often than not, these folks give selling a bad name and achieve little success. This strikes me as odd given the lucrative incomes that many sales professionals can and do earn, either equaling or greatly surpassing that earned by other professionals such as doctors and lawyers, who, by contrast, study and practice rigorously to earn their keep.

Sure, every now and then someone comes along and succeeds wildly in a sales career without any formal training. Then again, every few hundred years musical prodigies like Mozart come around. The rest of us would be well advised to prepare for success rather than hoping or wishing for success, and this preparation means practicing new skills. This is something I believe in fully rather than talking about hypocritically.

In my business, I practice and institutionalize every one of the methods and tactics described in this book. Sometimes it is not glamorous or sexy . . . more akin to the way the tortoise runs the race than the hare. But it works consistently and has *always* proved to be effective.

Using This Field Guide

My recommendation is for you to read through this field guide in the order it is written. There are several exercises for you to complete along the way, and completing these exercises accomplishes three things.

First, it requires you to demonstrate that you have grasped what you have read. If you haven't, then the subsequent materials become more difficult and won't be as clear to you. Writing your own answers allows you to think about what you have read and how you can apply it to the uniqueness of your selling situation. I have no way of knowing if your aim is to sell commodity products, high-value intangible services, big-ticket luxury items, and so on. The exercises allow you to take the tips, tools, and tactics described and adapt them to your particular products, services, and markets.

Second, it allows you to make an investment in the authorship of this book. In addition to my words on the page, the book becomes alive with *your* words on the page. Go beyond simply answering the questions to scribbling notes in the margins when you read something that excites, concerns, or inspires you.

Finally, by participating in the book, you will begin a process of planning for your own success. The elements of the process—reading, thinking, and responding—will all align to the goal that you are aiming for: improving your prospecting and business development effectiveness. You will begin thinking more about who your prospective customers are, what they want, and how you can ultimately get what you want by helping them to get what they want. Without even realizing it, your thoughts on prospecting and business development will become more serious, more planned, and more deliberate. You will be on your way to achieving your professional goals.

After you have completed your initial reading of the book, you should have an understanding of its contents. But the pages are still crisp, or if you are reading a digital copy, the screen still has few smudges. Over time, your goal is to smudge that screen, to weather those pages, as a result of referencing time after time the strategies and tactics you want to practice, hone, and improve upon. Each time you will add notes where you have been successful, where you have stumbled, and how you have adapted. It is, after all, a field guide, and not a leather-bound book that must never be removed from "Ron Burgundy's" bookshelf.

If you let it, this field guide will help you to become a more successful sales professional by unleashing the greatness that is already within you. But there is a catch, and it is an obvious one. Just as world-class golfers make golfing look easy, you probably falter considerably by comparison when you swing the sticks. That's because for most of us, golf is just playtime. Winning new business is where our income is earned . . . for many of us, it funds our livelihood.

If you want to earn enough to swing the sticks *and* to have the life you financially crave, the catch is that you need to take selling seriously. That means taking prospecting and business development seriously.

Wearing out the pages of *The CustomerCentric Selling Field Guide to Prospecting and Business Development* is the place to start.

My Key Takeaways

By completing the exercises in this field guide, I will accomplish these three things:

1.

2.

3.

Chapter 2

CustomerCentric Selling Primer

Whether you are an existing CustomerCentric Selling client or a salesperson not yet familiar with the CustomerCentric Selling approach, it is appropriate to take a moment to cover the core concepts of the CustomerCentric Selling methodology.

The main focus of *The CustomerCentric Selling Field Guide to Prospecting and Business Development* is to help individuals and organizations involved in sales *to become better, more effective prospectors and developers of new business*. Specifically, the aim is to help people move from traditional prospecting approaches and techniques to "customer-centric" behavior. It is my sincere belief that the CustomerCentric Selling methodology can help you become more customer-centric and therefore more successful.

The worldwide team at CustomerCentric Selling is engaged in the business of sales process improvement, Sales Ready Messaging, and sales training. The practical concepts within this book are the result of years of experience, research, and field testing—first as sales professionals ourselves, later as executives with increasing levels of sales management responsibility, and finally as leaders in a firm that has taught tens of thousands of customers to achieve better sales results.

As teachers, we work with all levels within client organizations. We help chief executive officers (CEOs) to learn how to take responsibility for their customers' experience and to shape them.

We teach sales executives how to own and manage their revenue engines.

We show marketing executives how to manage their content and create Sales Ready Messaging.

We teach first-line sales managers how to assess and develop the talent of their salespeople, manage a sales process, and *build a quality pipeline*.

Last—but certainly not least—we teach salespeople customer-centric behavior. In doing so, we focus on how to influence the words that sellers use when developing buyer needs for their offerings.

What Is Customer-Centric Behavior?

Customer-centric behavior has eight basic tenets. These are summarized in Table 2.1 and are explained in order in this chapter. As you read these descriptions, I invite you to imagine a spectrum of selling behavior ranging from traditional on one end to customer-centric on the other. Try to find yourself on that spectrum. Are you where you want to be? Are you as successful as you can be? If not, what needs to change?

Table 2.1 Eight Tenets of CustomerCentric Selling

Traditional Selling Behaviors	CustomerCentric Selling Behaviors
Make presentations	Converse situationally
Offer opinions	Ask relevant questions
Focus on relationships	Focus on solutions
Gravitate toward end users	Target businesspeople
Rely on product	Relate product usage

Traditional Selling Behaviors	CustomerCentric Selling Behaviors
Compete to stay busy	Compete to win
Close on the seller's timeframe	Close on the buyer's timeframe
Attempt to sell by: • Convincing, persuading • Handling objections • Overcoming resistance	Empower buyers to: • Achieve goals • Solve problems • Satisfy needs

Tenet 1. Having Situational Conversations Versus Making Presentations

Traditional salespeople rely on making presentations or doing product demonstrations, often using applications such as PowerPoint or using a member of the professional services or presales staff to perform the demonstration. Why? Because they believe that this approach gives them the opportunity to add excitement in the form of highly polished graphics, animation, and so on. It affords them the opportunity to turn down the lights and increase the dramatic effect of their presentations.

In successful selling we find that conversations are *far more powerful* than presentations. Your ability to *converse* effectively (have a meaningful two-way dialogue) is the key to your prospecting and selling success. And yes, it is possible to converse with audiences using PowerPoint—as opposed to presenting to them—but it is far more difficult. Have you ever had a conversation with a friend or a colleague that was based on a pre-scripted slide show? Of course you haven't, and so it shouldn't be a surprise that when senior executives see salespeople enter their offices with a laptop under their arm, many roll their eyes and sneak a peek at their watches.

When conducting sales calls, how often do salespeople dominate by doing the majority of the talking? Salespeople have their own agenda of what they would like to accomplish.

Good conversations require both parties to actively participate and exchange ideas. Sellers that do a great deal of telling and sharing opinions to have buyers draw the desired conclusions can be viewed as trying to manipulate the buyers.

Consider this: *In order to be effective, a salesperson must be able to relate his or her offering to the buyer in a way that will allow the buyer to visualize using it to achieve a goal, solve a problem, or satisfy a need.* This, in turn, requires a conversation. For a variety of reasons, though, only a small percentage of salespeople are able to converse effectively with buyers, especially executives and decision makers.

The CustomerCentric Selling Field Guide to Prospecting and Business Development aims to help you *engage* in relevant, situation-specific conversations with senior executives that have the ability to purchase your offering. It is phase one of the selling marathon.

By contrast, CustomerCentric Selling is a broad methodology designed to help you navigate the entire sales process with decision makers, without depending on canned slide presentations. In short, it can help you to become more effective and more successful.

Checkpoint #1

What are far more powerful than sales presentations?	
An effective salesperson will be able to relate his or her offering to the buyer by doing what three things? 1. 2. 3.	

Tenet #2. Asking Relevant Questions Versus Offering Opinions

Traditional salespeople offer their opinions to prospects, whereas customer-centric salespeople ask relevant questions. It is far more comfortable for buyers if sellers focus on asking versus telling. This allows the buyers to steer the direction of the sales call based on their own responses. It also allows the buyers to draw their own conclusions.

Another potential issue occurs when sellers attempt to develop a vision for a solution to their buyer's goal or problem *before* their prospective buyer does. When a traditional seller sees the solution, he or she tends to project that vision onto the buyer, saying things like, "In order to deal with that problem, you will need our seamlessly integrated software solution . . ."

When that occurs, what is happening on the other side of the table? Very often the prospective buyer is thinking something along the lines of "Oh, yeah? Do we now? Says who?"

People don't like loved ones telling them what they need, much less a salesperson with a motive and a mission! Most people, when in the role of buyer, would resent it when sellers try to control or pressure them.

People love to buy but hate feeling like they are being sold to. Buying means they are in control. Being sold to means they are being controlled, and few people like to be controlled.

At CustomerCentric Selling, we have found that top-performing salespeople use their expertise to frame interesting and helpful questions rather than deliver opinions. Asking *intelligent and relevant* questions shows respect for the buyers and engages them.

When buyers encounter a series of intelligent questions—questions that are on point and that can be answered, and the answers to which build toward a useful solution—they do not feel that they are being sold.

Asking Questions: Are You Up to the Test?

Write three to five questions you normally ask during a sales call.

1.	
2.	
3.	
4.	
5.	

Now, take a look at the five questions you have just written. Do traditional salespeople typically ask similar questions? What's your budget? What's your timeline? Do you have the ability to buy?

When asking questions similar to those, whose needs are you attempting to process, yours or the prospect's? Whose needs is the prospect interested in processing, yours or his or her own? Being customer-centric means focusing on the needs of the *prospect*.

Checkpoint #2

Rather than delivering opinions, effective salespeople do what?	
Asking intelligent and relevant questions does what?	

Tenet #3. Solution Focused Versus Relationship Focused

Traditional sellers are relationship focused, and customer-centric sellers are solution focused.

If the seller does not understand how the buyer will use the seller's offering to achieve a goal, solve a problem, or satisfy a need, he or she really has no choice but to fall back on relationships. Why does it happen? In many cases the answer lies in the training (or lack of) that the salesperson receives. Many organizations engage their product marketing department to teach salespeople about their products. Not surprisingly, the result is a sales force that can tell you all about the esoteric features of the products but can't tell you how the products are used or how the buyers can benefit from them. And the rare product marketers who do understand the uses of the products tend to have their understanding at the day-to-day user level, *not* at the decision-maker level.

Checkpoint #3

Rather than focusing on product features, you should do what two things?

1.

2.

Tenet #4. Targeting Businesspeople Versus Gravitating Toward Users

Traditional salespeople gravitate toward the users of their products, while customer-centric salespeople target business decision makers.

For Reflection

List the last five titles of prospects you have recently engaged with.

1.

2.

3.

4.

5.

| Of these titles or prospects, how many are actual decision makers? | |

The strength of traditional salespeople lies in talking about the features and function of their offerings, and users are the group most likely to be interested in or tolerate this approach. However, selling to the users is not the same as selling to a decision maker in a way that allows that individual to visualize the usage of the product to . . . achieve a goal, solve a problem, or satisfy a need. In order for salespeople to have the confidence to engage in a conversation with businesspeople, they must be prepared to engage in business conversations. A business conversation should be usage and results oriented, rather than feature oriented. It focuses on why the offering is needed; how it can be used to achieve a goal, solve a problem, or satisfy a need; and how much it costs to use versus what benefits it provides.

Most selling organizations give their salespeople "noun-oriented" product training—that is, they provide a great deal of information about the product's features but very little about how it is used in day-to-day applications. Not surprisingly, these organizations will gravitate toward hiring salespeople who are able to understand the product on that level—that is, as trained users—and then will reinforce that perspective. In other words, it is a vicious cycle: a suboptimal selling structure perpetuating itself.

Nouns Versus Verbs: Are You Up to the Test?

Write down words you commonly use to describe your offerings. Then place a checkmark for each under either "Noun" or "Verb."

Word Used	Noun	Verb

The cycle can be broken. The CustomerCentric Selling methodology maps out how marketing departments can make the transition from product training to product-usage training by creating Sales Ready Messaging for targeted conversations. This approach enables and empowers traditional sellers to target businesspeople and engage in customer-centric conversations.

Checkpoint #4

A business conversation should be what?	
In doing so, it focuses on what three things? 1. 2. 3.	
Should your sales messaging be noun oriented or verb oriented?	

Tenet #5. Relating Product Usage Versus Relying on Product

Customer-centric conversations take place when sellers are able to relate conversationally with their buyers about product usage. Traditional salespeople working for traditional organizations and using outdated product marketing approaches have no choices but to rely on their products to create interest. They educate buyers about products, assuming that the buyers can figure out for themselves how they would use them.

In some special circumstances, this strategy works, but only for a while. Here's a scenario you may recognize: A technology company introduces a hot new product. The company finds a guru to endorse the technology, writes a white paper full of snap and sizzle, hires a public relations firm, and wows a couple of technology trade shows. Sales take off.

But how much actual selling took place in this scenario? Were the salespeople helping potential customers visualize how they could achieve a goal, solve a problem, or satisfy a need by using the new technology? Or was this a case where the early-market buyers were sufficiently smart and innovative enough to figure out their own product usage through (or even despite) having a traditional product presentation?

So sales take off, and the people at the technology company come to believe that they are superior sellers and marketers. Then, mysteriously, sales plummet. What is happening here?

Geoffrey Moore's insightful book *Crossing the Chasm* (1991) and subsequent books highlight the difficulties that technology companies face when they run out of innovators and early adopters and then have to figure out how to *find new prospects*—targeted buyers who don't know they have a need for the offering and don't have a vision of how they would use it.

Customer-centric sellers succeed where traditional sellers fall short. The CustomerCentric Selling approach can help you and your selling organization become more customer-centric.

Checkpoint #5

Should sellers focus on product usage or product features?	
How do we define a prospect?	

Tenet #6. Competing to Win Versus Competing to Stay Busy

Traditional salespeople and their organizations focus heavily on quantity rather than quality when building pipelines. Salespeople may avoid asking tough qualification questions, fearing that the buyers may decide not to proceed with their evaluation and therefore the sellers' pipelines will have to be adjusted downward. The challenge lies in failing to ask these questions, and, as a result, buyers may decide to do business with another vendor or decide to make no decision because they never were qualified.

"Winners never quit and quitters never win" is an overused expression in sales organizations in an effort to justify attempts to hang on to every opportunity in the pipeline. Traditional sellers seem to embrace this expression. Yet, deep down there is a more valid reason for their approach. If they were to disqualify a sizable opportunity, they would proactively have to find another opportunity to replace it. In other words, they would have to prospect! If sellers are unable or unwilling to prospect for new opportunities, they will have a hard time deciding to walk away from a prospect, even if they know there is no real chance of closure.

Superior sellers enjoy two major advantages when it comes to disqualification. By initiating buying cycles at higher levels, they find that those buyers do not want to waste their time nor their staff's time. Therefore, it has to be a mutual decision that allocating resources is worthwhile. Competent salespeople also place a high value on their time and recognize early signs that they don't have a fair chance at winning and decide to withdraw.

Of course, it is important for companies to pay attention to their cost of sales, but we suggest taking a slightly different approach to recognizing the expense of going the distance in the sales marathon— and ultimately losing. If you subtract your average win rate from 100 percent and multiply it by your total cost of sales, you will arrive at an important figure: *the cost of competing and losing.*

What is *your* cost of competing and losing?

$$100\% - \underline{\hspace{3cm}} \times \underline{\hspace{3cm}} = \$\underline{\hspace{3cm}}$$
$$\text{(avg. win rate)} \quad \text{(total cost of sales)}$$

To sum up the difference as it relates to allocating time, consider that an unsolicited RFP (request for proposal) is delivered to salespeople from two different companies. The first is a "B Player" who anxiously reads it, decides it looks like a good fit (despite the fact that another vendor wired it), and willingly spends hours to respond, with a win rate below 5 percent. But when an "A Player" receives an RFP, he asks for access to the buying committee, and if denied, he will most likely decide not to submit a bid. The time spent by the B Player responding and losing could be allocated to finding better (more winnable) opportunities.

Checkpoint #6

Should you focus on quantity or quality when building your pipeline?	
What two major advantages do superior sellers reap with disqualification? 1. 2.	
How do you calculate your cost of competing and losing?	

Tenet #7. Close on the Buyer's Timeline Versus the Seller's Timeline

Suppose you know a salesperson who has been working on a major opportunity for the last three months. You ask when he believes it will close, and he provides a date. Let's assume you also know the buyer or the decision maker and have the ability to ask her when she believes her company may be ready to buy, and she provides a date. Whose date do you think will be earlier? Our bet would be that the seller's date would almost always be sooner.

Salespeople and sales organizations are under pressure not only to generate revenue but also to do it consistently on a monthly, quarterly, and annual basis. This often causes close dates to be based upon which vendor wants or needs the order without regard for when the buyer will be ready.

In turn, this fractures relationships, as decision makers feel pressured when asked for orders prematurely. If sellers push too hard, they can lose the sale. Often the best result is getting the order at any cost, which usually requires that the seller offer a discount to motivate the buyer to order sooner than he or she would otherwise have desired. Frantic quarterly or year-end closes smack of traditional selling. If continued on a regular basis, buyers become trained (by the sellers) to purposefully delay decisions until the end of the month or quarter.

Would it not be more sensible to incorporate how and when the buyer wants to buy into the sales process? Very few A Players have the ability to look at an opportunity as a buy versus a sales cycle; if they did, sellers would see a way to merge the needs of the buyer to make a decision in conjunction with what a seller needs in order to make a detailed recommendation. Those steps can be agreed upon, so that both parties can reach a mutual deadline. This also gives a buyer or buying committee some control over the process.

Checkpoint #7

If you do not sell based on the buyer's timeline, what do you risk?	
If you view opportunities as a buy cycle instead of a sell cycle, you will be able to do what?	

Tenet #8. Empower Buyers Versus Attempting to Sell Them

When we ask salespeople who attend our workshops to define *selling,* we are always astounded at the perception salespeople have of their own profession. For example, they define *selling* as convincing, persuading, getting someone else to do what you want, handling or overcoming objections, taking a least five noes before giving up, negotiating to get what you want, and—of course—the big one: closing. ABC—always be closing. Close early! Close often!

Looking at this list and thinking about the mindset behind it, it is no wonder that most people—even salespeople—do not like being approached by salespeople.

Interestingly, we also work with buyers; and when asked to describe salespeople, most buyers use terms like *aggressive, pushy, manipulative, overfamiliar, prone to exaggerate, poor listeners,* and so on. When asked to narrow down these negatives to one word, the number one response we get from buyers is *pressure.* When buyers deal with sellers, they feel pushed, manipulated, and pressured into doing things that they end up wishing they hadn't done.

These preconceptions are traps. If sellers are going to avoid them, they will have to learn how to sell differently. Their concept of selling will have to be reframed so that it becomes customer-centric (again, empowering buyers to achieve a goal, solve a problem, or satisfy a need). This is not all that difficult to accomplish. We say that because we have taught thousands of self-declared "nonsalespeople" how to sell. By *nonsalespeople,* we mean people who do not want to think of themselves as salespeople in the traditional sense—engineers, accountants, lawyers, consultants, scientists, and the like.

Think about the engineer who is a nonsalesperson, for example. Engineers love to help people solve problems. By and large, engineers do not want to behave like traditional salespeople, but when the concept of selling is reframed, they are very happy serving as customer-centric salespeople. By no means can all engineers be taught to sell, but there are a number of them who have a positive mindset, have few preconceived notions, and are open to the opportunity. One of the challenges of working with bright, well-intentioned engineers is breaking them of the habit of telling buyers what they need (despite the fact they are usually right) and getting them to slow down, practice some real patience, and remember to ask buyers questions so that the buyers can arrive at their own conclusions.

We believe a seller's objective when prospecting and attempting to engage with a buyer should be to help the buyer achieve a goal, solve a problem, or satisfy a need—and then be prepared to leave if the seller doesn't believe that the prospect can be empowered to accomplish one of those goals. This may sound like only a small shift away from a traditional prospecting and sales approach, but in fact it is fundamentally different. Imagine yourself as a buyer. Wouldn't you rather have a meeting with someone who had that customer-centric attitude, rather than the mindset of a traditional salesperson?

Even A Players Can Improve

Over our careers we have met a number of truly gifted A Players, or natural salespeople. They make it look easy. On a consistent basis they achieve 200-plus percent of quota, though most of them cannot define what makes them successful. A 2008 survey performed by Sales Benchmark Index (see the figure below) showed that on average within organizations 13 percent of the salespeople generate 87 percent of the revenue. On a statistical basis, we've concluded that 13 percent of sellers qualify as A Players.

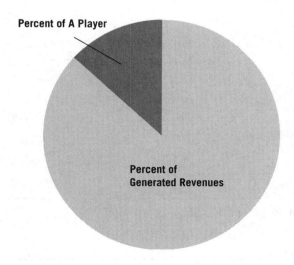

If you look back at the eight tenets we have just discussed, these A Players are consistently customer-centric in regard to the first six tenets. This is why A Players are successful.

But in our experience, even those A Players have room for improvement with the seventh and eighth tenets. Most A Players believe (like their less skilled peers) that selling is convincing, persuading, and so on. So we believe even the most gifted sellers can become more customer-centric. We further believe the key to a player's success as a sales manager is to first become consciously customer-centric.

The eighth tenet is one that is more difficult to implement unless organizations embrace the concept: *empower buyers versus attempting to sell them*. While we would be naive to say that companies won't have any tightwire acts at the end of a quarter, it shouldn't be the norm.

Later in this book, I will show a way for salespeople, sales managers, and marketers to use all these tenets to influence their approach to prospecting and business development, so keep reading.

Checkpoint #8

What is the number one most common word that buyers associate with sellers?	
A seller's objective when attempting to engage with a prospect should be what four things? 1. 2. 3. 4.	
Instead of "selling" your prospects, you should do what?	

Chapter 3

WHAT IS PROSPECTING?

Important statistics to remember: 92 percent of
C-level executives never respond to e-mail blasts or
cold calls, but 84 percent of prospects do respond
when referred by coworkers or customers.

The word *prospecting* is short business slang to describe the act of searching for prospective customers. It is an essential component of the selling process, for without prospects, there would be no customers.

Not everyone engaged in selling is required to engage in cold-call prospecting, a process in which the seller has to identify a potential buyer, make contact, and, the hope is, get the buyer to engage in a discussion. Some of the people engaged in selling, most notably retail store salespeople or inside salespeople, are presented with prospective customers when people walk in the door or call in. Yet what salespeople do from that point onward will determine the success of their selling efforts, and so this book will prove to be a very helpful guide to selling successfully for all sellers.

For most salespeople, however, and certainly for those who aspire to higher earning positions, the art of locating and engaging prospects is a critical part of the job. In a way, it is what you are being paid so handsomely for: finding prospects. Granted, the real goal is to develop mutually beneficial relationships that help customers to achieve goals, solve problems, or satisfy needs while rewarding your company with substantial revenues; but you will find the likelihood of these outcomes to increase as you practice the tips and techniques within these pages.

What Prospecting Is Not

As we define what prospecting is, let's also be clear about what it is *not*.

1. Prospecting is not passively waiting for the phone to ring, hoping for a prospect to call.
2. Prospecting is not an inquiry or lead generated by marketing, a website, or a trade show.
3. Prospecting is not sending out a friend request on Facebook or LinkedIn.
4. Prospecting is not easy.
5. Prospecting is not another person's or department's job, because your income is too important to leave that to chance.

Prospects are not "things." They are, for the moment, faceless and nameless people with needs, wants, feelings, and desires, just like you. To be a world-class salesperson, you need to become a world-class prospector, and that means honing your skills of determining where to prospect for customers, how to quickly identify them, and how to earn their trust.

Years ago my sons gave me a fly-fishing outfit for Father's Day. You know—pole, reel, waders, flies, the works. The problem was, while I was interested in fly-fishing, I knew nothing about it. We lived in Colorado and were surrounded by beautiful mountain lakes and streams. It was a mecca for fly-fishing.

Not knowing anything about fly-fishing, I signed up for a two-night "instructional class" offered by the Colorado Free University. Ironically, something was explained to me the first night of class that has helped me in my sales prospecting efforts.

The instructor explained that while we have all these wonderful lakes and streams, you first have to be able to see trout in the lake or stream before you even think about putting your fly in the water. Simply stated, if you can't see fish, you probably won't catch anything. You are wasting your time.

Why is this significant? Companies within your marketplace are the "lakes and streams." They may look promising; however, there has to be someone, an individual, within those companies that has a goal, problem, or need that has to be addressed and that you can help address. You have to be able to see fish! As salespeople, our goal is to find the prospects within those companies.

As you will see later in this book, social media platforms such as Facebook, Twitter, and LinkedIn can (and should) be used effectively as a tool in the prospecting effort, but simply using them to "friend" others does not constitute prospecting. Prospecting requires the collection and use of intelligence about targeted buyers, just as fly-fishing requires knowledge of which streams to place your fly in and what particular fly will be of interest to the fish you are attempting to catch. Once you have collected intelligence about an opportunity (such as the triggering events I will discuss in later chapters), you will consider using specific methods to have informed and relevant conversations with prospects you have targeted.

Five Myths of Prospecting

Now that you know what prospecting is not, let's turn our attention to five of the most common myths of prospecting.

Myth #1. Prospecting Is Selling

Just as marketing is closely linked to but different from the sales function, so too is prospecting a separate function from the sales process. *Prospecting creates opportunities. It leads to selling.* The job of prospecting is to find qualified leads that may have the ability and incentive to buy your product. In a way, prospecting is simply discarding all the unqualified suspects and retaining those who are looking to achieve a goal, solve a problem, or satisfy a need. Only after this process is complete, should the selling begin.

Myth #2. Prospecting Is Only a Numbers Game

Prospecting is much more than merely a numbers game. Traditional approaches to prospecting for business relied on contacting large numbers of cold contacts. However, quality supersedes quantity. You must carefully identify and target individuals that have a need to evaluate and buy your product or service. I will show you how to do this as we continue.

Myth #3. Scripts Are for Kids

Many salespeople insist on prospecting without any script or defined messaging. Defined messaging provides the framework of a successful prospecting campaign. It allows you to test what *high-probability* goals, problems, or issues are important to the individuals on your Targeted Conversation List. "Winging it" is not the way to go if you want to work efficiently and effectively and, most important, be able to identify which approaches work best and which ones don't.

Myth #4. Prospecting Takes Too Much Time

Like anything else worthwhile, prospecting does take time, but it takes too much time only if you fail to plan, prepare, and apply what you will learn in this guide. It should only take a few minutes to determine if the person you have engaged has a goal, problem, or need that he or she wants to address. Don't waste too much time with people with a nice job title but without influence. Sure, they may be able to provide you with some intelligence, names, issues, etc., but remember this: *you can't sell to someone who can't buy.*

Myth #5. Close Them on the Appointment

Too many reps focus on scheduling an appointment or, worse yet, a demonstration. Next thing you know, the appointment is canceled via e-mail. When you attempt to follow up, the person won't take your call. She goes ice cold. Surprise, surprise.

Prospects will sometimes find it easier to agree to your request rather than telling you they are not interested. If prospects are remotely interested, then you will want to pursue a more subtle approach by processing their needs and not yours. I will show you later in this book how you can simply state that you'd like the ability to learn more about their operation and what they are trying to accomplish. Help them (don't *get* or *force* them) to admit a goal, problem, or need. After all, without a goal, you don't have a prospect.

Checkpoint #9

What is the real goal of prospecting?	
True or false: Prospecting is a lead generated by marketing.	
Prospecting can lead to what?	
You do not have a prospect without what?	

Six Traits of Highly Successful Prospectors

Highly successful prospectors exhibit six important traits:

1. *Process orientation.* Successful prospecting doesn't just happen. It requires careful planning and preparation, and then it requires actively applying the principles you will learn in this book. Salespeople who recognize this and make it part of their daily activities are more likely to succeed. This includes determining to *whom* you are selling; what *their goals, problems, or needs* are; *what you have* that can help them; which *Sales Ready Messaging*

would cause them to engage; which *methods* you will utilize to deliver that message; and how *frequently* the message is delivered.

2. *Optimism.* You have to believe that despite all the noes and rejections you will receive, you will find people or organizations that have a goal, a problem, or an issue that they would like to address and be willing to discuss with you.

3. *Resilience.* A rejection of your message should not be taken personally. Of course, you have probably heard this before, but it is true. Maybe it was the message, or maybe it was the approach. Either way, if it is not working, then you will need to examine what you have done and try another message or approach, and this book will give you the knowledge to do just that. As I mentioned previously, this is another reason why you want to use carefully crafted scripts. It allows you to track and determine what works and what doesn't, and with what job titles.

4. *Instincts.* Successful prospectors have the ability, when engaged with prospects, to know whether they are generally interested or are simply placating the salesperson. Based on this sense, the prospectors can determine whether this "opportunity" warrants an investment of their valuable selling time. After all, time is all they have, and they know how valuable it is. They'd rather take their time helping prospects that share goals, problems, or needs *and* have the authority and incentive to address those.

5. *Intuition.* Successful prospectors also demonstrate the ability to find and create opportunities where none appear to exist. They scrutinize situations, events, news stories, annual reports, and press releases for "triggering events" and can identify where their offering plays and what potential value it brings. For this reason, a significant section of this book is devoted to understanding and capitalizing on triggering events.

6. *Persistence.* Highly successful prospectors understand that it will take time to gain "mindshare" and establish their competency. They have the ability to do this, not by being offensive but by sharing interesting and valuable information that engages the prospect and piques his or her interest.

What Is CustomerCentric Prospecting?

CustomerCentric Prospecting is a modern prospecting system that helps salespeople to focus on contacts within prospect organizations that are most receptive to receiving a phone call or e-mail from them by:

- First, placing themselves in their prospect's shoes
- Being well informed about the prospect's business goals, problems, and needs
- Planning their approach and follow-up
- Reaching out at the right time with the right Sales Ready Message
- Utilizing technologies that allow them to be more effective and productive

Checkpoint #10

	True	False
1. Prospecting is waiting to receive a phone call or e-mail from a prospect.		
2. Prospecting is responding to a lead generated by marketing.		
3. Prospecting is easy; anyone can do it.		
4. Prospecting is another person's or department's job, not mine.		
5. Prospecting is simply sending out friend requests on Facebook and LinkedIn.		
6. Prospecting requires the collection of information about the targeted buyer.		
7. Prospecting creates opportunities. It leads to selling.		
8. You must carefully identify and target individuals that have a need to evaluate and buy your product or service.		
9. Prospecting scripts allow you to test which high-probability goals, problems, or issues are important to your prospects.		

Continued on next page

Continued from previous page

	True	False
10. Like anything else worthwhile, prospecting takes time, planning, preparation, and action.		
11. Prospects find it easier to agree to a salesperson's requests than to tell the salesperson they are not interested.		
12. Prospecting is a business process, a series of steps.		
13. Scripts allow you to track and determine what works and what doesn't, and with what job titles.		
14. Successful prospectors have the ability to find and create opportunities where none appear to exist.		
15. Customer-centric prospectors focus on their prospects' goals, problems, or needs.		

Answers: 1–5 are false; 6–15 are true.

Chapter 4

Planning—The Six Steps to Prospecting Success

Step 1. Timing

Almost as important as where to begin is *when* to begin.

Let's say that you were thinking you were going to rely on last year's carryover and it is the end of January and nothing has closed. You are then late to the party. The reality is that if you haven't closed anything in January, you are going to have to close twice as much in February just to make year-to-date (YTD) quota! That's a tall order even for the most accomplished salesperson.

The time to begin developing your Territory Sales Plan is right *now*. Get started by analyzing your current situation.

Step 2. Analysis

What is it that you know, or don't know, about your territory, your products, and your existing customers; and what do you and don't you know about what will be required of you as a salesperson? This is the time to gather all the reconnaissance you can. Some of the information I'm recommending that you analyze may not be readily available to you. That's okay; go to the keeper of that information and get it. Potential sources are your sales manager, finance, sales operations, and marketing.

You will want to analyze:

- *The current-year compensation plan.* What are you required to generate in revenue? Where does the company want it to come from (products, existing customers, new-name business)? Will you be paid differently for different types of business? Will you have complete ownership of the customer you sell, or will you have to give the customer up after some period of time? This helps you begin to focus on where you need to be spending your time, when, and for how long.
- *Your YTD performance.* Since we don't always have the opportunity of starting at the beginning of the selling year, sometimes we have to jump right in! Having said that, where are you YTD against your compensation plan and sales goals? Are you ahead of goal or behind? By how much? What do you need in the next month, quarter, to be where you need to be, or where do you need to be to take advantage of any accelerators in your compensation to purchase that new car, pay off that credit card, etc.
- *Your win rate.* What is your win rate? When you are all in, when you are competing to win, what is your win rate? When I ask this question in my workshop, I'm consistently shocked at the number of salespeople who can't answer this question. Just like hitting and on-base percentages are key performance statistics for professional baseball players and pass completions are key numbers for professional quarterbacks in the NFL, so too is the win rate a key performance statistic for professional salespeople. Unless you are an independently wealthy lottery winner, you will need to depend on the sales profession to enable you to fund your lifestyle. Consider this example for a moment. If you have a 50 percent win rate and win one out of two opportunities you compete for, that means your pipeline has to be *twice* as large! If your pipeline is not twice as large, you will have to have a win rate greater by

twice than 50 percent! I don't know anyone who has a 100 percent win rate.

- *Seasonality.* Take a look at you and your company's sales history. Are some months better than others? Are some months very slow? Attempt to figure out why. Ask people who might be able to give you some insight. What can you do to capitalize on those buying months? What can you do to entice your prospects in those slower months? Just as prospects use the end of your quarter to gain more favorable pricing, you can use the end of each quarter, or business events within the quarter, as a reason to engage. For instance, let's say your offering allows your prospect to comply with some mandatory quarterly reporting requirement or to automate some report that is being produced and filed manually on a quarterly basis. Some salespeople would elect not to engage at that time due to what they feel is their prospects' preoccupation with reporting and compliance. I believe just the opposite. I think this creates an opportunity for a proactive prospector. The ideal time to attempt to engage might just be while prospects are hard at work complying. You might challenge them to continue to operate the way they are operating, to remain at risk, to incur additional expense, to be exposed to fines—*or* to engage with you now. Knowledge of your market, your prospects, and their goals, problems, and needs is essential. Will you need to step up your prospecting and business development activities?
- *Discounting.* What impact did or does discounting have on your overall revenue performance? Are you discounting to simply "buy business," or are you getting something of value in return, like a larger sale, more seats, a longer term, referrals? If you are required to close 10 new pieces of business this year in order to make quota and you discount each by 10 percent simply to buy the business, that means at the end of the year you are going to have to find, sell, and close at least one additional piece of business to make quota. It's hard enough to find the first 10; do you really want to give revenue away and have to find another opportunity to work? Think about it.

- *Vertical markets.* Are there vertical markets in which your company has done very well? If so, you may want to leverage the names and successes of those companies within those verticals. Are there vertical markets where you haven't made significant inroads but you think you should? What are they? Who are the Key Players? What are the top three goals, problems, or needs that those Key Players are struggling to address? How do those goals, problems, and needs manifest themselves? How do you find out about them? Besides reviewing your company's records and speaking with your manager, sales operations, or marketing, simply take a look at your company's current client list. Are your clients categorized using SIC (Standard Industry Code) or some other method? If so, you should be able to sort or locate reoccurring codes to identify markets where you company has enjoyed success and then attempt to exploit it. When I first started selling human resource information systems years ago, I went into our marketing supply room where we kept all our sales collateral—printed brochures, data sheets, success stories, etc. I found three success stories developed around existing customers: a hospital, a luxury hotel, and a savings and loan. In addition to identifying each business as vertical, the success stories educated me about the goals, problems, and needs that caused these companies to evaluate and purchase my employer's offering. I leveraged those success stories to target hospitals, luxury hotels, and financial institutions, and I used the goals, problems, and needs to develop my sales ready messaging. What do you have in your product or service offerings that would allow your prospects to address those goals, problems, or needs?
- *Your existing pipeline.* What does your existing pipeline look like? Is it strong enough or large enough to support the amount of revenue you are required to generate? Here is an example of what I mean. If you have a 50 percent win rate (you close one out of two opportunities you compete for) and you are required to close $1,000 in new business this month, then you need to have at least $2,000 in your pipeline, at the *E* (Evaluating) stage (this stage is explained in Chapter 5) in order to even potentially

make your number. Does that make sense? I'll go into more detail about calculating pipeline strength later in this chapter.

- *Product offerings.* What do you have to sell? What products do you have, or what do you have within those products, that your competitors don't? I'm talking about unique features and capabilities. Why is this important? What do you want your prospects to want—those things that are unique to your company and its offering or those same things that they can get from everyone else in the market? I'm asking you to consciously think about your strengths and how you can exploit them.

- *Your personal income requirement.* Finally, how much do you want to earn this year? Unlike other people who may receive their obligatory 3 to 5 percent annual increase, we as salespeople have the ability to impact our own earnings. We can look at our compensation plan and calculate exactly what we need to sell in order to make the money we want to make. So let me ask you, what do you want to make this year?

- *Existing customers.* That's right, prospecting and business development should be undertaken with existing customers. The relationship already exists. It's much easier to sell new and additional products to an existing satisfied customer than it is to try to unseat an incumbent competitor in a company you have never done business with before. So who are your existing customers? What products or services do they currently have, and what ones don't they have? Do they need what they don't currently have? Whom should you attempt to engage in order to begin a sell cycle for those products they don't have? Why would they want your product? What bad thing will or could happen to them if they don't have it? Think about how you would position it with them.

To demonstrate what I mean, in Table 4.1 is an example of a simple opportunity matrix that I have created that lists the names of eight of our clients and our product offerings. I've placed an X under each of the service offerings that the clients have purchased or participated in. Take a look at the matrix and tell me what you conclude.

Table 4.1 Opportunity Matrix

Client Names	Product Offerings				
	CCS*	PBD†	CCM‡	SPM§	CCR¶
Recondo Technology	X			X	X
Altia	X			X	
Peoplefluent	X	X		X	
Darryl Flood	X	X	X	X	
Knovel	X		X	X	X
Reval	X		X	X	
Knowlagent	X			X	X
Solutions-II	X	X		X	X

*CustomerCentric Selling Workshop
†Prospecting and Business Development Workshop
‡CustomerCentric Messaging Workshop
§Sales Process Management Workshop
¶CustomerCentric Selling Refresher—"What do you do when . . . ?" Workshop

Have you reached any conclusions? Let me share with you mine. It shows me that all the clients who have trained their salespeople in CustomerCentric Selling have also trained their sales management team by having them participate in the Sales Process Management Workshop. However, besides showing me what they have purchased, what they haven't purchased, and what I might potentially speak with them about, it also indicates to me that I may want to develop entire prospecting campaigns to promote our two newest product offerings to the entire client base: the Prospect and Business Development Workshop and the CustomerCentric Selling Refresher Workshop. I know that 76 percent of these clients haven't participated in the Prospect and Business Development Workshop, 50 percent haven't scheduled a CustomerCentric Selling Workshop for their sales team, and only 24 percent have participated in the *free* CustomerCentric Messaging Workshop that we offer to our clients' marketing personnel. It's our investment in our clients' continued success

Exercise 1. Opportunity Matrix

To assist you in analyzing your existing client base and gathering your thoughts, I'd like you to take a moment to complete the following opportunity matrix worksheet. If you don't want to use the one I have provided here, you can take a lined piece of paper or use Excel if you prefer, using the example in Table 4.1 as your model. In any case, at the top of the worksheet, make a list of your product offerings; there's enough space to list 10 different products or services. Once you've listed your clients and your product offerings, place an X where the client and a product offering purchased by that client intersect.

Client Names	Product Offerings									

Continued on next page

Continued from previous page

- What is the most utilized product?
- What is the least utilized product?
- What existing clients deserve your attention?
- What product(s) would benefit from a targeted prospecting campaign?
- What percentage of your client base do you think would purchase the underutilized product? Best case and worst case?

The client relationship already exists. Use this analysis and newfound information to begin to exploit it.

Step 3. Goal Setting

Using the analysis of your customer base, prospects, and revenue requirements, you need to establish goals for what you need to accomplish. Things to consider include:

- How many wins do you need in order to make your revenue quota? A simple way of establishing that would be to take your annual revenue requirement divided by the average dollar value of the sales or transaction. That will provide you with the *number of estimated wins* you will need to close this year.
- How many of those wins do you want to come from existing clients? How many wins from new-name business? Are you compensated differently on one versus the other?
- What about getting referrals from existing clients? Would you like some number of new clients to come from referrals? If so, you can wait for them to spontaneously appear (doubtful), or you can proactively go obtain them.
- What new products can you identify for existing customers? What do you sell that they don't have?
- What existing or underutilized products can you sell to new and existing customers? Can you achieve greater penetration with the complete product line?
- How many wins do you want by each quarter? By month? By week?
- Based on your win rate, how many leads will you need to generate your new-name business goal?

You will find you do much better if you take the time to write down your goals; they become the cornerstone of an annual business plan.

Step 4. Strategies

Now that you have established your goals, how do you intend to achieve them? In addition to your individual lead-generation efforts and your responses to inbound inquiries, do you have any particular growth strategies for your territory? Here are some ideas to consider.

- Are there particular verticals, projects, or situations where you have experienced greater success and you would like to build upon that success?
- Do you want to enhance your mix of business (new-name accounts versus existing accounts)?
- Are trends emerging in the marketplace that align with your offering?
- Can you identify sales ready messages that resonated with your prospects that you want to exploit?
- Do you wish to increase account penetration with core products?
- Will you build your social network database and expand the use of referrals?

Step 5. Tactics

Identify the top 10 prospects carried over from the previous year:

- Out of the top 10, identify the top 5. These are the ones that you feel are your very best.
- Prepare a tactical plan to convert each of those five prospects to "E" status. How will you reengage with them? What, by mutual agreement, are you going to do, and when, to bring them to closure?
- Schedule "refocus meetings" to recap goals, reasons, and the prospects' solution. Let's get the wrinkles out of the sheet! Schedule a meeting to confirm what it is that you know; find

out what you don't know; and have the prospect confirm what specific capabilities that they are going to need from you in order to achieve their goal, solve their problem, or address their needs.

- Attempt to measure the cost of doing business today and confirm the value to the prospects' organization. I'm amazed at the number of salespeople who don't take the time to understand the value of their offering to their prospect. It's the logic that supports the emotional decision to purchase your offering. It's the rationale that allows your prospect to seek and obtain funding versus focus on other projects. When your prospects are teetering on the top of the sales funnel, it's what gives them the courage to dive in. If you have attended a CustomerCentric Selling Workshop, then you know that the price of your offering pales in comparison with the value your prospect will derive from purchasing it.

- Document the results via a sales process control letter. Don't leave things up to the prospect or your recollection; document and confirm what it is that you have been able to find out and how you have agreed to move forward.

- Share the results with your manager. Two heads are better than one. Your manager might be able to give you some insights that you haven't considered and, if your manager is doing his or her job correctly, provide you with the skills and opportunity coaching necessary in order to move this opportunity to closure.

Prospecting and New-Business Development

You have begun to develop your prospecting and business development plan. You've *analyzed* your performance, your markets, your pipeline, your product offerings, and your customer base, and you've even looked at your compensation plan in detail to determine how you can use its provisions to achieve your own personal income requirements. Based on that analysis, you've set some goals for yourself and developed some strategies to *achieve* those goals. It's not enough to think, "I'd like to generate more business," or "Of this year's business, 50 percent will come from my existing customer base." How are you going to make it happen? This is a point in your planning process where your actions *must* speak louder than your words. You need to think about *what you are going to do tactically* to execute against those strategies that will give you the greatest chance of achieving your goals.

- *Set aside sacred prospecting time.* At a *minimum*, I suggest that you set aside 25 percent of your workweek: 10 hours a week, 2 uninterrupted hours per day, dedicated strictly to prospecting. Put it on your daily calendar. Let's say that every morning from 10 a.m. to 12 noon is your sacred prospecting time. During that time you are not checking or responding to e-mail, not accepting inbound telephone calls, not doing any other work . . . you are executing your prospecting and business development plan. No interruptions. You'll respond to the e-mails and phone calls when you are done at or around noon.
- *Build your pipeline to the optimum strength to meet your revenue goal.* Everyone seems to take this tactic at face value. However, do you know how big (opportunities and value of each opportunity) your pipeline needs to be in order to achieve your revenue quota? Do you know what your average transaction size is? If you do, based on that average transaction size, how many pieces of business do you need to close or win in order to meet or exceed your quota? And finally, based on your historical win rate, how large does your pipeline need to be at any point to ensure that you meet your quota? If you were able to answer these questions, congratulations! If you weren't able to answer them, why not? I'd like you to obtain the greatest return on your investment of effort and time. It's time to get serious. In the next chapter, I'll introduce you to a few simple calculations that you can use to calculate your pipeline requirements.
- *Identify specific technologies you will use to enhance your productivity (LinkedIn, iLantern, Salesforce.com, ConstantContact, Lead411, etc.).* There are new technologies that allow you to execute many of the things that we suggest that you do in this field guide—and that let you do them more efficiently. They give you back valuable prospecting and selling time. In Chapter 6, I'll introduce you to some of these new applications.

- *Identify specific existing accounts and specific new-name accounts that you will pursue based on your strategies.* Let me give you an example using existing accounts. In the opportunity matrix I shared with you earlier, I identified eight companies and the particular CustomerCentric Selling offerings they had participated in and *not* participated in. The matrix showed me that I had potential with existing accounts to sell our Prospecting and Business Development Workshop and our CustomerCentric Selling Refresher Workshop. Tactically, I'm going to pursue those companies with those offerings.

- *Identify what specific method(s) you will use in order to engage with prospects (referrals, referrals via social networking, telephone, e-mails, direct mail, etc.).* These are just some of the methods that are available to you and that we will instruct you how to use in this field guide.

- *Create the specific sales ready messages that you will use to cause people to engage.* There are business reasons (goals, problems, and needs) why individuals spend their company's money to buy your offering. What are those reasons? Where are people having difficulty? What might be happening in your marketplace that would cause them to look for help? And how will you position them in such a way to create curiosity and interest? In Chapters 7 and 8, we will provide you with ideas, instructions, and tools that you can use.

- *Determine in what order you will use your sales ready messages and with what frequency.* What goal-, problem-, or need-related sales ready messages do you want to lead with? How much time will you give people to respond? If the targeted individuals don't respond, what will you say next and how will you say it? You don't want to be a nuisance, but you do want to obtain mindshare.

- *Use multiple methodologies in parallel.* As we have already suggested, there are multiple methods for delivering your sales ready messages and engaging with your prospects. As you read this guide, you'll find that there is research that has been conducted to determine what methods are most effective in getting a senior executive to engage with a salesperson. There is also research that indicates even a minimally effective method, for example cold calling, when paired with another minimally effective method, e-mail, can dramatically improve the results of your prospecting efforts.

Step 6. Plan Execution

With everything I have suggested, and everything you are already doing, how do you put it all in play? How do you accomplish everything that needs to be accomplished? Just by executing against the first five steps, you'll find that you have the potential for putting more order in your workday and getting back more time to do other things. However, be that as it may, I'd like to offer you some suggestions:

- *Create a tactical calendar with dates and steps or tasks to be accomplished.* I am going to recommend that you use the task reminder feature in your SFA (sales force automation) or CRM (customer relationship management) application or any other project plan application you might currently use to make sure that nothing falls between the cracks. You want each task and due date specified.
- *Give yourself ample time to execute each step in your plan.* All too often in their zeal to get started, salespeople get overly aggressive with their plan. They try to do too much, too soon, and too fast. Other unanticipated things come along that cause them not to follow their plan or that result in them failing to complete some tasks, and the next thing you know, they have abandoned their plan. Make your plan manageable. Make your plan somewhat flexible.
- *Establish success metrics and measure your plan's performance.* You'll want to measure the effectiveness of your plan and its tactics. I don't want you to become overly consumed with record keeping, but think about things you might measure. For example, let's say that you begin to execute a five-step prospecting plan to contact 25 executives over a 10-day period or 2 business weeks.

You want to see at which step in the plan you obtained the greatest result.

- At what step did the executive engage? Was it the first attempt, second attempt, etc.?
- What sales ready message did you use at that step that caused the executive to engage?
- What issues seem to be creating the most interest?
- What method was most effective—e-mail, phone call, phone call followed instantaneously by an e-mail, etc.?
- What was the least effective method?

  By doing this you can begin to determine what method works and what method does not. What message is most effective? This information allows you to modify your plan, methods, and message. You want to do and use those things that allow you to obtain the most favorable result, and you don't want to waste your sacred prospecting time on those things that simply are ineffective. The only way to know is if you establish some success metrics and begin to measure your plan's effectiveness.
- *Monitor your plan performance on a weekly basis.* If you go for, say, a month without looking at your plan performance, you may have squandered three weeks doing the wrong or ineffective thing. Look at your plan weekly; then monitor and adjust your plan and tactics based on what you learn. Be critical of your own performance. You'll find it sharpens your skills.
- *Evaluate your pipeline strength on a weekly basis and adjust your prospecting plan and activity level based on your pipeline strength.* I have suggested that you dedicate, at a minimum, two hours a day to prospecting and business development in an effort to build your pipeline to optimum strength. If you look at your results on a weekly basis, you may see that you need to increase your activity. For example, imagine closing a couple of nice pieces of business—and simultaneously losing some opportunities that you were counting on. All of a sudden your pipeline is not even close to where it needs to be! By reviewing your pipeline strength on a daily basis, you can determine if you need to invest more

than the two-hour suggested minimum. You want to continue to have new prospects enter the top of your sales funnel.

- *Watch for new and unexpected opportunities (trends, new requirements, issues, emerging markets, etc.).* Think about this for just a minute. What could happen in your marketplace that would cause an organization to potentially purchase your offering, and what bad thing happens to that organization if it doesn't? Let me give you an example based on my marketplace—sales performance improvement.

On a daily basis I receive automated alerts to earnings reports filed by companies. I'm specifically looking for public companies that have missed their earnings projections due to a decline in revenue. Missed earnings projections due to a decline in revenue represent an opportunity for me to engage with that company's CEO, CFO, COO, and SVP of sales. If they don't address the revenue issue, it could result in a decline in stock price, loss of confidence by consumers, pressure from aggressive competitors, loss of market share, loss of confidence in executive leadership, etc. These are all things that I could potentially exploit using carefully crafted Sales Ready Messaging.

We will discuss in more detail what those things might be, how to become alerted to their existence, and when and how to use them in Chapter 7.

- *If something is not working, do not be afraid to change or modify your plan.* I've told you that you need to monitor your performance on a weekly basis and suggested some reasons why; and I have directed you to establish some success metrics to determine what is working or not working. Simply stated, if you find your plan isn't working, then it is time to consider changing your plan. You need to be continually analyzing and evaluating your plan in an attempt to make it more effective.

- *Plan your work; work your plan.* It is easy to become distracted by other important things that require your attention and by other things that are easier and more pleasurable to do. Developing prospects and business is hard work. It's what leads to *selling.*

Checkpoint #11

What are the 10 things you should consider when performing your prospecting analysis?

1.

2.

3.

4.

5.

6.

7.

8.

9.

10.

What way could you calculate how many wins you would need to make your quota?	
Where should you start once you have formulated your prospecting strategy?	
What is the minimum percentage of your workweek you should spend prospecting?	

Chapter 5

PIPELINE ANALYSIS

Step 1. Calculating Pipeline Strength— What Do You Need to Make Quota?

During my discussion of the planning steps, I referenced a couple of times the importance of building your pipeline to *optimum strength*. The next obvious questions are (1) what do you mean by *optimum strength*? And (2) how do you calculate your pipeline requirements?

Let's deal with the first question. If you have a $1 million annual sales quota, *at a minimum* you need to generate $1 million in potential sales opportunities. When you factor in your win rate, say 50 percent—in other words, you win one, you lose one—it means you need to generate at least $2 million in opportunities and take them through the entire sales process. Does that make sense? You are going to need twice as much in your pipeline.

Now let's address the second question. How do you calculate your pipeline requirements? In order to do that, there are a number of variables that you need to consider:

- "Normal" time spent at each milestone (expressed as a percentage of the total average sales-cycle length)

- Average length of sell cycle (expressed as the number of sales cycles in a year)
- Probability of closing a prospect at each milestone (use the CustomerCentric Selling standard percentages until a history of actual close percentages are built)
- Annual quota
- YTD quota
- YTD actual
- Average sale or transaction size

Pipeline Milestones

Before we proceed any further, I think it is necessary to explain the pipeline milestones that will become part of our calculations. If you are a CustomerCentric Selling practitioner, this is simply a review of what you already know—a refresher. If you are new to CustomerCentric Selling, pipeline milestones are used to specify where a particular opportunity is in the sales process. Unlike some subjective grading systems, the milestones are not based on a salesperson's opinion, nor are they simply a record of activity. They reflect *auditable progress* through the sales cycle. The figure that follows outlines the five CustomerCentric Selling pipeline milestones: Inactive, Active, Goal Shared, Champion, and Evaluating.

To help understand the terms in the figure, note that:

- *Inactive* means that a targeted account fits a company's target market and is assigned to a salesperson, but there is no current activity. A salesperson's business development effort should focus on getting a buying cycle started by getting a targeted Key Player within the account to share a goal, which would advance it to the next milestone.
- *Active* indicates that contact has been made and some form of interest on the part of the customer or prospect has been expressed.
- *Goal Shared* is the initiation of a sales cycle in CustomerCentric Selling; it indicates that a targeted Key Player has shared a desire to achieve at least one goal that is on the menu of business issues the seller can help the Key Player address.

CustomerCentric Selling® Pipeline Milestones

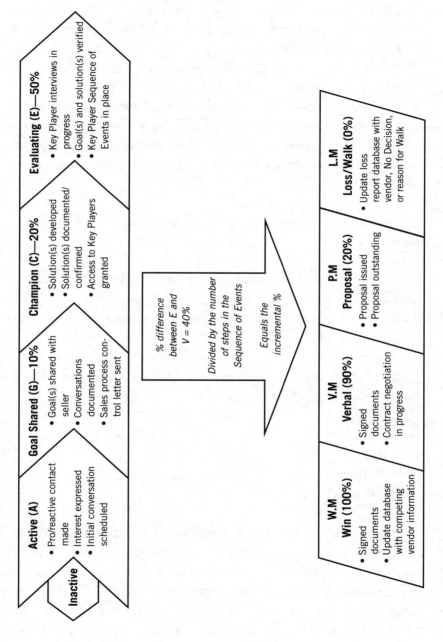

Active (A)
- Pro/reactive contact made
- Interest expressed
- Initial conversation scheduled

Inactive

Goal Shared (G)—10%
- Goal(s) shared with seller
- Conversations documented
- Sales process control letter sent

Champion (C)—20%
- Solution(s) developed
- Solution(s) documented/confirmed
- Access to Key Players granted

Evaluating (E)—50%
- Key Player interviews in progress
- Goal(s) and solution(s) verified
- Key Player Sequence of Events in place

% difference between E and V = 40%

Divided by the number of steps in the Sequence of Events

Equals the incremental %

W.M
Win (100%)
- Signed documents
- Update database with competing vendor information

V.M
Verbal (90%)
- Signed documents
- Contract negotiation in progress

P.M
Proposal (20%)
- Proposal issued
- Proposal outstanding

L.M
Loss/Walk (0%)
- Update loss report database with vendor, No Decision, or reason for Walk

- *Champion* status can only be conferred by the sales manager. It happens only after all the qualification elements have been achieved; the letter, fax, or e-mail has been sent; the buyer has agreed to the content; and the buyer is willing to provide access to Key Players. The sales manager must have reviewed the customer document and given it a "Champion" grade, usually after a brief discussion with the salesperson.
- *Evaluating* status is determined by the sales manager, but only after the salesperson has gained consensus from the Key Players that further evaluation of the salesperson's offering is called for and after a Sequence of Events has been accepted by the buying committee.

Opportunities remain at this stage until one of three things happens:

1. The buyer withdraws (and the opportunity becomes a loss).
2. The seller withdraws.
3. The seller asks for the business after the Sequence of Events has been completed.

Once the seller has asked for the business, the opportunity goes into one of four pipeline grades:

- W (win)
- L (loss)
- V (verbal)
- P (proposal)

You will notice in the previous figure that I have assigned "probabilities of closure" to each one of the pipeline milestones. They represent the probability of an opportunity at that particular grade ever turning into a win. For example, you can see that "Goal Shared" is 10 percent, meaning that only 1 out of 10 opportunities that reach this grade and stage in the sales process will turn into a piece of business. These are baseline probabilities. Your probabilities will change once you begin tracking and measuring your conversion performance. But for the purpose of the following exercises, we are going to use these baseline probabilities.

Step 2. Calculating the E-Pipeline Requirement

Most of us have one year in which to achieve our annual quota, and so let's assume a salesperson has an annual quota of $1,800,000. That means that on a monthly basis, he or she is going to need to close $150,000 in business ($1,800,000 ÷ 12 months = $150,000). The average sales cycle is considered to be 3 months. That means that every 3 months—in other words, every quarter—this salesperson has to close $450,000 in business ($150,000 × 3 months = $450,000). Now here is where the probability comes into play. The probability of closing an E, when a Key Player has agreed to evaluate, is 50 percent, meaning that one out of two opportunities will probably turn into a win. And this means this salesperson will have to have twice as much in his or her E pipeline every quarter in order to meet the revenue requirement ($450,000 × 2 = $900,000 × 50 percent probability of a win = $450,000). What I'd like you to do now is take a moment to fill in the right-hand side of Exercise 2 and calculate your E-pipeline requirement.

Exercise 2. Calculating Your E-Pipeline Requirement

Calculation Variables	Example	Your Information
Annual quota	$ 1,800,000	
Monthly quota (annual quota ÷ 12)	$ 150,000	
Average length of sales cycle	3 months	
Probability that an E-opportunity will close	50%	

Continued on next page

Continued from previous page

Calculation Variables	Example	Your Information
Revenue needed during one sales cycle (monthly quota × average length of sales cycle)	$450,000	
Factor to adjust E-pipeline target (1 ÷ decimal equivalent of the % probability)	2	
Factor times revenue for sales cycle	$900,000*	

* The E pipeline for salespeople who are YTD against quota is $900,000. Any shortfall must be multiplied by the factor and added to the pipeline target.

Step 3. Defining and Calculating a New Opportunity

Another outcome of your prospecting and development efforts will be to generate new opportunities. In order for you to build your E pipeline to the "optimum strength" to support your revenue requirement, you are going to have to bring into the top of the sales funnel some number of new opportunities to ensure that you are able to build your pipeline to the required strength.

A *new* opportunity is defined as an opportunity entering the pipeline for the first time as a result of a successful sales call, achieving at least the "G" milestone. A potential status change could be:

From I to G with qualified _____ agreed upon
From A to C with qualified _____ agreed upon
From A to E with qualified _____ agreed upon

An I or an A is *not* an opportunity and should not be included as such in any pipeline health calculations.

Now that we have determined what constitutes a new opportunity, let's determine how many new opportunities, at a *minimum*, you need to generate as a result of your prospecting and business development activities to build your pipeline to optimum strength.

Let's look at a different example. Suppose a salesperson has a $900,000 *annual quota* and an *average transaction size* of $350,000. That means our salesperson will have to close 3 transactions annually ($900,000 ÷ $350,000 = 2.6, or [rounded up] 3 transactions) in order to achieve his or her quota.

When you divide the number of wins needed annually by the probability of closing a G (Goal Shared), which is 10 percent, that means this salesperson is going to have a minimum of 26 prospects admit a goal on an annual basis. When you divide 26 by the 12 months in the year, you find you must, on average, generate two new opportunities each month.

Exercise 3. Calculating New Opportunities

If you believe that sales is a numbers game, let's calculate how many new opportunities, at a minimum, you will need to generate in order to support your pipeline.

You've just been given your assigned quota for the year. How many new opportunities, Gs, are you going to need to add to your pipeline on a monthly basis to build your pipeline to optimum strength and achieve quota? Use the table below to calculate your new opportunities.

	Example		Your Information	
1.	$900,000 (annual quota) / $350,000 (average transaction size)	= 2.6 wins needed annually		
2.	2.6 (wins needed annually) / 10% (probability of closing a G prospect)	= 26 new Gs needed annually		
3.	26 (new Gs needed annually) / 12 (number of months in a year)	= 2.2 (rounded down to 2), the number of new Gs needed monthly		

Continued on next page

Continued from previous page

As you perform this exercise, you are most likely somewhere other than January 1 in your selling year. You likely have calculated your new opportunity requirement and have closed some business; now you have to determine how many additional new opportunities (Gs) you are going to need to build your pipeline to optimum strength. Use the table below to calculate your additional opportunities needed.

	Example			Your Information	
1.	$$\frac{\$300,000}{\$350,000}$$	= 1 (number of additional wins needed annually)			
2.	$$\frac{1 \text{ (number of additional wins needed annually)}}{10\% \text{ (probability of closing a G prospect)}}$$	= 10 (number of additional Gs needed annually)			
3.	$$\frac{10 \text{ (number of additional Gs needed)}}{8 \text{ (number of months in the sales cycle or number of months left in the selling year, whichever is greater)}}$$	=1.25 (number of new Gs needed monthly). Add this total to the total from the previous exercise.			

Total Original Gs Needed	Number of Additional Gs	Revised New Gs Needed	Total Original Gs Needed	Number of Additional Gs	Revised New Gs Needed
2	+ 1.25	= 3.25			

While these simple calculations are not meant to compute the coordinates to land NASA's lunar lander on the moon's Sea of Tranquillity, they do allow you to calculate:

- How many pieces of business you must close annually to meet your sales quota
- The minimum number of new opportunities (Gs) you will need to generate on a monthly basis to support your sales quota

- When below quota, how to calculate how many additional new opportunities, above the minimum, you are going to need to add to your pipeline in order to attain your sales quota

These calculations allow you to balance the strength of your pipeline against your prospecting activities.

Checkpoint #12

What are the five pipeline milestones?

1.

2.

3.

4.

5.

Continued on next page

Continued from previous page

What are the four pipeline grades?

1.

2.

3.

4.

How do we define a new opportunity?

Chapter 6

PREPARATION

By failing to prepare, you are preparing to fail.
—BENJAMIN FRANKLIN, U.S. STATESMAN

Imagine trying to coach a team to a championship game victory without reviewing game films or developing a plan of attack—or in the spirit of a field guide, trying to hike up and through the Himalayas without supplies, a map, or training. We all recognize how foolish and dangerous those activities would be; yet when it comes to how to earn a living to fund our livelihood and provide security for our families, far too many salespeople treat preparation with the same level of disrespect. I believe that Benjamin Franklin was correct when he said, "By failing to prepare, you are preparing to fail." However, if *you* become one of the few who does prepare to win new business, then you will have a decided and sustainable advantage over your colleagues and competitors.

Let's get down to brass tacks. Here are the steps to take in order to be prepared for successful prospecting:

1. *Build a prospect database (companies).* If you haven't already done so, you will want to identify those organizations that meet your marketing criteria—industry or vertical companies, revenue, number of employees, location, etc. If this information is not readily available, it may be purchased from list vendors, manually researched, and developed; or use many of the SAS (software as a service) applications that can allow you to specify your needs and export them into your SFA or CRM application.

2. *Determine job titles (think "sell, fund, and implement").* Whom do you need to be selling to? Salespeople become enamored with job titles. They end up attempting to sell to people with a title but without power or influence. This is a perfect time to look at your sales history for the successful sales. See who signed your agreement, who approved the funding, and who was responsible for the implementation or activation. This is a starting point to set your target.

3. *What are they dealing with that would make them want to speak with you?* We have already established the first core concept, *no goal, no prospect.* There has to be a reason for someone to change how he or she is currently operating. What do you know to be an *actual reason* and what *logical assumptions* can you make based on your company's knowledge of the market? Can you glean them from customers you have helped, issues and trends based on conversations with prospects, and the state of the market? You are looking to identify high-probability goals, problems, and needs that you are able to help your targeted organization and job titles address.

4. *What is a triggering event?* The definition of the term *triggering event* depends upon what you are selling: missed earning, fines, lawsuits, new-product announcements, declining profitability, leadership changes, mergers, business expansion, government directives, etc. They can be found through conversations with prospects, press releases, news stories, annual reports, analyst meetings, websites, government reporting, and so on.

5. *Develop Sales Ready Messaging.* You need to have the tools to approach and *engage* with your prospects. I'm talking about

menus of goals, Solution Development Prompters that align with the goals, supporting success stories, e-mail messages, and phone scripts.

Let's take a look at your *conceptual* sales territory. I'm not talking about your territory literally; I'm asking you to look and think about your territory conceptually. We have always believed that the targeted organizations within your territory, however that is defined, fall into one of the following two categories: *looking* or *not looking*. However, through our research and experience, we've since identified a third category that sits right in between the two.

I call that category the *point-of-need* category. An organization in this category has just experienced a triggering event, something that will require the organization to change how it operates; the event, though, is so new or current that the organization hasn't begun to look just yet. The organization is hurt, wounded, *in need*, and is not sure what to do. This creates an opportunity for an astute and intuitive salesperson.

From a prospecting perspective, I'm going to need to engage with each category—the not looking, point of need, and looking—a little differently!

Utilizing Technology

In addition to your company's SFA or CRM, there are a number of specialty applications that by themselves, or integrated with your SFA or CRM, can aid the salesperson in gathering information about potential prospect organizations and delivering Sales Ready Messaging to them. Some of those products are:

- *Lead411 (http://www.lead411.com)*. Lead411 is an information services company that provides businesspeople with executive information, company information, and news about these companies. The executive information delivers verified phone numbers, biography information, and executive e-mail addresses. Company data include industry information, business addresses, yearly revenues, number of employees, job openings, and company descriptions. Daily news alerts serve as sales triggers that produce timely sales leads for clients and include stories like venture capital news, acquisitions, and new hires.

- *ConstantContact (http://www.constantcontact.com).* Constant-Contact is a web-hosted e-mail marketing service that allows businesses to stay connected to their customers and prospects via e-mail, surveys, and event marketing. This service can send thousands of e-mails at one time and maintain status reports.

- *LinkedIn (http://www.LinkedIn).* LinkedIn is a well-known business-oriented social networking site. It has more than 160 million registered users, spanning more than 200 countries and territories worldwide. LinkedIn claims to register two new users per second. Users can identify companies, job titles, individuals, and special interest groups; receive news alerts; and request referrals via individuals in their LinkedIn network.

- *InsideView (http://www.insideview.com).* InsideView aggregates information about companies, executives, and related events (news, blogs, SEC filings, job listings, social network data) for approximately 700,000 North American companies and 200,000 top international companies. This information comes from a variety of structured and unstructured content sources such as Reuters, Jigsaw, LinkedIn, and many others. InsideView also parses news and information from approximately 20,000 web-based news publications, Twitter feeds, and blogs. It helps subscribers generate sales leads, qualify those leads, and use technology tools to help find big sales opportunities for customers.

  I discovered this application when doing research for our Prospecting and Business Development Workshop. I became so enamored with its capabilities that we began subscribing to it for our own prospecting and business development use. You can register for a free limited-use version on InsideView's website. CustomerCentric Selling clients who would like to subscribe to InsideView for use by their sales organization receive a 10 percent discount.

- *iLantern (http://www.ilantern.com).* iLantern automates the best practices in prospecting. Using proven technology to scrape the web for content (news, corporate website, social media, etc.), iLantern distills those data to sales triggers that drive dramatic increases in response rates to sales and marketing efforts. Whether it's through a mobile device, Outlook, CRM, or marketing automation, iLantern quickly integrates into existing processes. For CustomerCentric Selling clients, iLantern automates the complete prospecting process, from finding sales triggers, to distilling them to those that are most relevant, to aligning the correct sales message to those triggers, to executing the e-mails within Outlook, to finally tracking that activity within the CRM.

Here is another application I discovered when doing research for our Prospecting and Business Development Workshop. It integrates with your existing prospect database, monitors those prospects to find triggering events, and allows you to target prospects with carefully developed and aligned Sales Ready Messaging via e-mail. CustomerCentric Selling clients who subscribe to iLantern also receive a 10 percent discount.

What Motivates Mainstream Prospects?

What motivates mainstream prospects to engage with a salesperson, to consider changing how they are currently operating? In order to get prospects to engage and begin a conversation about their goals, problems, or issues, you are going to need to say something that creates curiosity and interest. Let's face it—your prospects are being inundated by e-mails and phone calls from other vendors who want to talk about the features and functions and the speeds and feeds of their offerings. So how do you differentiate yourself from the masses? Research indicates there are four potential motivators. Because we don't always know which particular one will create interest and curiosity, we need to be prepared to capitalize on all of them when we can.

Fear of Potential Consequences

Did you know that people place three times more emphasis on loss than they do on gain? Think about that for a moment. Think about all those vanilla marketing messages that your prospects are being inundated with, such as "How would you like to improve . . . ?" Granted, people would like to improve, but why? Is it because they are losing something? Is it fear of potential loss that's motivating them to change?

Let me share with you a personal example that demonstrates this point. During the recent financial crisis, I was continually checking my investments to see how they were performing. As long as I was obtaining a marginal return, even though I didn't like it, I was content to leave my money alone. As soon as I was no longer obtaining that marginal return, as soon as one of my investments started losing its value, what did I do? I began looking for some other place where I could invest my money to once again begin earning a reasonable return. I was living with a marginal return and not liking it, but as soon as my investment began to lose, I decided I needed to take action. Again, people place three times more emphasis on loss than they do on gain.

That fear of potential consequences can also be attributed to your prospects failing to act when they know they should, or inertia. Sometimes people seek the safest and least disruptive route, the route that they know.

Politics Within the Prospect Organization

People who have the ability to buy what you sell occupy the positions they do in order to solve problems. They were not placed in those positions simply to "hold the reins." Additionally, no senior executive wants to be known as the source of problems. Staff meetings are not fun, especially when you and your organization are the subject of the meeting. Pressure from superiors, pressure from ambitious subordinates, and pressure from other parts of the organization can often be a catalyst for change.

Curiosity About the Actions of Peers

It's natural to be curious about what other individuals with the same job title and in the same industry are doing. Think about it. Regardless of how successful we may be in our jobs, we have a natural curiosity about what the other salespeople we work with are doing. Why is it, even in what appears the worst of times, there are some salespeople who consistently meet or exceed their sales quota? We can use that natural curiosity to our advantage.

Ego

In addition to being curious, senior executives tend to be competitive by nature. They want to be perceived as thought leaders; they want to be regarded as highly successful and impactful.

Look at all these items and think about why you are reading this book or contemplating attending our Prospecting and Business Development Workshop. If you are a salesperson, manager, or senior executive, you are reading this book for one or more of the above reasons.

Exercise 4. Prospect, Job Titles, and Menu of Goals

Are you ready to practice what we have discussed so far? For the purpose of this exercise and the application of what you have learned so far, let's get started by working with a single company. We'll use the company you have selected for this exercise for all the remaining exercises so that you can see how everything has its place and all the concepts fit together. Here is what I'd like you to do:

Targeted Company		
Step 1	Select a single company that you would like to do business with—a company that you've had no contact with and that meets your marketing criteria. Enter the name of the company in the right-hand column under the heading "Targeted Company."	
Targeted Conversation List		
Step 2	Determine the job titles of the three senior executives that you are going to need to speak with in order to get your offering sold, funded, and implemented. Now write those job titles in the numbered spaces provided, under the heading "Targeted Conversation List."	1. 2. 3.

Continued on next page

Continued from previous page

Menu of Goals		
Step 3	Finally, select one of the job titles from the Targeted Conversation List and circle it. For that particular job title, I'd like you to think about the business issues that keep that particular job title up at night—three high-probability issues that could be addressed by your offering. Enter those three issues in the numbered spaces provided under the heading "Menu of Goals."	1. 2. 3.

So here is what you have done. You have identified a *company* that you would like to do business with; you have selected the *job titles of the three executives* that you believe you are going to need to speak with in order to get your product sold, funded, and implemented; and for one of those job titles, you have identified *three high-probability issues* that you could help them address with your offering if they are experiencing any of the three issues.

It's about the business—your prospect—and what the business is experiencing that would motivate it to engage with you. Remember, *no goal, no prospect.*

Checkpoint #13

What are the five steps for preparing for successful prospecting?

1.

2.

3.

4.

5.

What are the four drivers that motivate prospects?

1.

2.

3.

4.

Complete this saying: "No _____,
no prospect."

Chapter 7

ENGAGING AT THE *POINT OF NEED*

People encounter "events" in their lives that represent change. Often these events require investment, major decisions, and changes in how a person or company operates. On a personal level, this includes leaving home to go to college, getting married, having children, buying a home or moving across country, putting kids through college, retirement, and so on. You can probably see how each stage or event equates to change—and very likely investment or expense.

The same is true in business. After all, businesses generally go through life phases just as people do. These phases include growing from a one-person bootstrap start-up to leasing a large facility, building out a management team, upgrading the management team as the business grows, expanding operations or product lines, growing geographically or through mergers and acquisitions, and, it is hoped, reaching a level of stability and moderate growth. Your objective, if you want to win business, is to identify key "triggering events" that represent a change and that position you and your company to help the prospect to navigate that change to a successful outcome.

What Is a Triggering Event?

A *triggering event* is an event whose consequences are so significant that it would cause an organization to:

- Examine and consider changing how it currently conducts business
- Adopt new behaviors
- Consider new ideas
- Pursue new opportunities

Generally, triggering events fall into one of three categories:

1. *Bad experience.* The prospect has a bad experience with a product or service, with people, or with a provider. For instance, there may have been a change in a product or service that created strong customer dissatisfaction.
2. *Change or transition.* The buyer experiences a change or transition in people, places, or priorities. For example, there may have been a change in executive leadership.
3. *Awareness.* The buyer becomes aware of the need to change for legal, risk-avoidance, or economic reasons. New regulations that change how an organization must operate and report, resulting in legal or financial consequences for noncompliance, is one example of this category.

Some examples of triggering events include:

Financial

- Earnings—below or above expectations
- New financing
- IPO—going public

Marketing and Sales

- Name changes or changes in positioning
- New products

- New markets
- New or lost customers
- New or lost sales channels or partnerships

Organizational

- Merger or acquisition
- Personnel changes
- Expanded hiring or layoffs
- Corporate relocation

External

- Laws or regulations
- The competitive landscape
- Customer trends
- Technology

Significance of Triggering Events

While triggering events may represent change, tension, and even chaos within a company, don't shy away from those that cause chaos and turmoil. They represent an opportunity for you as a salesperson if you recognize them and can help your prospect to successfully manage the change. How?

The event may indicate that the status quo in an organization is changing. Someone in the company—the hope is that it is your prospect—has a new goal, problem, or need that he or she has to address. Therefore, it is immediately pertinent to the individual you are trying to reach. Given this significance, action is required *now*, not later—*Now!*

Most salespeople, including your competitors, don't recognize the opportunity. Nor do they understand how to use the triggering event in their favor. This advantage allows you to develop timely and *relevant messaging* in a personalized manner that is aligned to the specific needs of your prospects. As a result, you will end up with two advantages:

1. You will be the first to identify the opportunity and help your prospect, which enables you to help define the parameters of the project—in your favor, of course.
2. By the time a competitor recognizes the opportunity or has been called in for a comparative bid, the prospect will have invested substantial effort in building a trusting relationship with you, giving you the edge.

How to Find Triggering Events

You can research new business opportunities based on triggering events, for little to no cost, by leveraging press releases, websites, and newswires. To begin using triggering events:

1. Review 10 to 15 of your recent sales wins and look at the goals, problems, or needs that prompted clients to buy your offering.
2. Research what you believe to be the sources of information: websites, press releases, annual reports, etc.
3. Remain alert and vigilant. You do this by using many of the technology tools we reviewed earlier, including InsideView, Google Alerts, LinkedIn activities, and Lead411.
4. Utilize an online system that will monitor your targeted company lists and automatically alert you to the types of triggering events you believe will provide you with an opportunity to engage.

How to Use Triggering Events

Understand the implications of triggering events and know what to do once they happen.

Once you have identified those triggering events that would create an opportunity for your offering, you have the ability to proactively reach out, using multiple prospecting methods, with messaging that is aligned with what is important to prospects.

Remember, prospects are not concerned about what you are selling or what you are trying to accomplish. They are concerned about what is important to them. Your understanding of the triggering event and its potential implication is what will allow you to craft a compelling message and encourage prospects to engage with you.

Here's a real-life scenario. You are monitoring the PRNewswire, and you see that First Software, one of the companies that you have on your list of targeted companies, has hired a new vice president of sales. What does this mean?

There Is a New Sheriff in Town

Think about it. Most often, a newly hired vice president of sales is in that new position because the old vice president of sales had some performance issues and not because he or she was promoted to CEO. The new vice president of sales has been hired to fix problems and improve sales performance. This person may have about 60 days to develop a plan to fix the problems he or she inherited. To take advantage of the situation, you'll need to recognize the following undercurrents.

Relationships Are Disrupted

When there is a new vice president of sales executive, preexisting vendor-client relationships are disrupted, perhaps even terminated. We know how difficult it is to unseat an incumbent vendor, a competitor. Now, it may have just been done for you!

Other Salespeople Fail to See It

Some salespeople view a change as a reason not to attempt to engage, thinking that the new person might be too new, unfamiliar with what he or she inherited, etc. In CustomerCentric Selling, we see it completely opposite. We view this as an *opportunity*.

Personal Ego

As we pointed out in Chapter 6 in the section "What Motivates Mainstream Prospects," ego is one of the main motivators. A new vice president of sales has been hired to work with an underperforming sales team and fix problems. People facing these challenges are looking to make a name for themselves. They are looking for help, and they are likely willing to explore something new.

Identifying Triggering Events

In the next exercise, I'd like you to identify triggering events—events that your prospects could experience—that would create an opportunity for you to sell them your product or service. These are things you want to be watching for or be alerted to. Table 7.1 is an example that I have created for a vice president of sales. The left-hand column lists the *goals, problems, or needs* that senior sales executives continually find themselves struggling with—and that CustomerCentric Selling is capable of helping them address. The center column specifies how those goals, problems, or needs might manifest themselves: the *triggering events*.

Table 7.1 Triggering Events

Job Title: Vice President of Sales		
Goals, Problems, or Needs	**Triggering Event**	**Sources of Information**
• Not meeting revenue goals • Inaccurate sales forecast • Excessive discounting • Little or no prospecting • Increasing losses to competitors • Losses to "no decision" • No defined sales process • Inability to converse with senior executives • Long start-up times for new salespeople • 13% of the sales team generating 87% of the revenue • Difficulty demonstrating value • High turnover • Increasing cost of sales • Excessively long sales cycles	• Change in sales leadership • Missed earnings reports • Competitor wins • Decline in stock prices • Analyst alerts • Hiring or recruiting salespeople	• Press releases • Competitor press releases • Analyst reports • Missed earnings reports • Websites (client and competitor) • Client lists • Sales jobsites (open positions)

You can see in Table 7.1 that I listed a "change in sales leadership" as the number one triggering event. Think about it. Any sales organization that continues to have the goals, problems, or needs that I have listed in the table, without correcting them (inertia), will probably require a change in sales leadership. That is an opportunity for me to engage with and help the new vice president of sales to identify and address the organizational sales difficulties that he or she has inherited. Logical, isn't it?

In the right-hand column in the table are some sources of information that I can monitor and check to identify those triggering events that are important to me.

Now, it's your turn. I'd like you to use the information that you developed in Exercise 4 (in Chapter 6) to fill out the table in Exercise 5.

Exercise 5. Identifying Triggering Events

Step 1. Using the table provided below, insert the job title of that one senior executive on whom you wanted to focus your prospecting efforts.

Step 2. In the left-hand column, under "Goals, Problems, or Needs," begin by entering the "Menu of Goals" items from Exercise 4. Feel free to add any additional goals, problems, or needs that you can think of.

Step 3. In the center column, "Triggering Events," I want you to think about how those business issues could potentially manifest themselves.

Step 4. In the right-hand column, "Sources of Information," make a list of potential sources of triggering events.

Step 1. Job Title:		
Step 2. **Goals, Problems, or Needs**	**Step 3.** **Triggering Event**	**Step 4.** **Sources of Information**

Many years ago I did some consulting work for a small environmental company in Denver, Wixel Environmental. Wixel sold a product that allowed companies to comply with EPA regulations governing the labeling, storage, and transportation of hazardous materials. Each month the EPA would publish a report, available to the public, which listed all the violators, identified their violations, and specified the financial penalties they were assessed. Wixel used this information to identify its prospects, knowing what it needed to do to align its *sales ready messaging* and understanding what the financial implications and benefits were to a company complying with the regulations. This is a perfect example of using triggering events to engage with prospects at their time of need.

Here is what you have now done: for a Key Player, you have identified triggering events that can be addressed by your product or offering, and you have identified where and how you can find that information.

While it is not impossible to monitor all the sources of information you have identified, it would certainly take a tremendous amount of time. However, here is where technology can come into play and maximize your productivity. Applications such as LinkedIn Updates or Google Alerts routinely report some of this information. iLantern (http://www.ilantern.com) and InsideView (http://www.insideview) can monitor thousands of sources of information for you and alert you to only those triggering events that you have identified and requested. They are both fabulous productivity tools for salespeople.

Checkpoint #14

How do we define a *triggering event*?	

What are the three categories that triggering events can fall into?

1.

2.

3.

A triggering event may indicate what?	
Where should you start to find triggering events?	
Understanding the triggering event and its implication will allow you to do what?	

Chapter 8

SALES READY MESSAGING

The purpose of this chapter is to introduce you to the Sales Ready Messaging tools that we believe should be developed for the sales team's use. Many of the tools I'm going to introduce you to in this chapter are not needed for prospecting and business development; however, they are part of the overall CustomerCentric Selling sales process. I think it's important to know what they are, what their purpose is, how they are developed, and where they all fit. If you are an existing CustomerCentric Selling client, this will serve as a review. If you are new to CustomerCentric Selling, you'll quickly learn that a salesperson who is prepared and has the proper tools is likely to be more professional, knowledgeable, and successful.

At its best, selling consists of a series of conversations with buyers. I personally believe that the ability to converse effectively with a senior executive must be the salesperson's number one skill. If you can't converse effectively, you will be outsold by the salesperson who can.

During these conversations, the salesperson's objective is to uncover and understand the buyer's goals, problems, and needs. Throughout this process, the salesperson learns about the buyer's circumstances, and, as a result, the salesperson can begin to position his or her company's offerings. An additional benefit of a competent diagnosis is that the root causes of why the buyer cannot achieve a goal, solve a problem, or satisfy a need are clarified.

Selling organizations benefit greatly from influencing and steering these conversations. But this seems like an impossibly ambitious and far-reaching objective—so ambitious, in fact, that most such organizations that have considered it have dismissed it out of hand. In this chapter, allow me to put forth a strategy to accomplish that goal.

No, you can't anticipate all potential interactions with buyers at all levels. You can't "boil the ocean," as the saying goes. So our approach is to help the salesperson orchestrate conversations with targeted decision makers and influencers about specific business issues addressable with his or her offering. After having a buyer share a goal, we help the salesperson follow one of a number of flexible scenarios.

Looking at this issue from another perspective, we can see that companies that fail to step up to the challenge of influencing sales conversations are abdicating an enormous degree of responsibility, relinquishing it to their salespeople. They are asking their salespeople to interpret and communicate the capabilities of their products single-handedly. As a result, a 20-person sales team could have 20 or more different ways, some effective, some ineffective, of describing its offering to the market.

So let's begin with the three conditions that must exist in order to have an effective sales conversation about an offering:

1. The buyer's title (or function) and vertical industry must be known.
2. The buyer must share a business goal or admit a business problem.
3. The seller's offerings must have capabilities that a targeted buyer can use to achieve a goal, solve a problem, or satisfy a need— and, of course, the seller must understand and articulate those capabilities.

Given these three conditions, we believe organizations can help their traditional salespeople have these kinds of sales conversations.

They can create Sales Ready Messaging—a way of approaching a conversation that greatly increases the chances of success.

How to Develop Sales Ready Messaging

How to develop all the Sales Ready Messaging tools that I'm about to introduce is not the purpose of this chapter or this field guide. However, it is important to discuss their development and use because much of the information we've discussed and you have practiced in some of the previous chapters will be required by marketing to complete these tools.

To begin developing your own Sales Ready Messaging plan, you need to consider the following question:

> What are the typical job titles or job functions of the decision makers and influencers with whom you have meaningful conversations?

Or phrased slightly differently,

> Who is in a position to buy, fund, and implement your products and services?

In Exercise 4 in Chapter 6, you identified a company that you wanted to target. For that company, you made a list of the job titles of the individuals that you are likely going to need to engage with who can buy, fund, and implement your offering. This may be one title or many, since in some instances, such as enterprisewide selling situations, salespeople must engage with a number of people who influence and affect the outcome.

After you listed the titles that you will likely target, you answered the next question:

> For each of these job titles, what goals or business objectives should they have in that function? Which of those goals are addressable through the use of your offering?

Each goal in your list was one that your company's offering can help the prospect to achieve. Try to focus on goals that have a monetary component so that later the financial benefit of achieving the goal can be cost justified and the cost-benefit can be calculated and demonstrated.

Telephone Scripts

When we mention scripts, we often get comments like "I don't need or like scripts." The fact of the matter is that all prospecting begins with a script. By beginning with a script, we are able to track and determine its effectiveness by both job title and issue, modify them according to the results received, and make them better and more effective each time we use it. So having said that, I'd like you to develop a library of telephone scripts, a series of scripts, based on what you are trying to accomplish:

- Initial issue-based contact (see Table 8.1)
- Initial contact following a triggering event
- Initial contact when referred
- Follow-up on a previous call or e-mail

Examples of Telephone Scripts

Here is a very effective issue-based prospecting script that can be delivered in about 8 to 12 seconds. What we will try to do in that 8 to 12 seconds is to create some interest and curiosity about how we:

- Helped someone else with the same or similar job title
- Deal with a high-probability issue that we believe our prospect is also struggling to address

In order for this script to work, the *job title* and the *high-probability issue* have to be aligned; this issue has to be important to the job title. In this particular case, forecasting accuracy is a constant challenge for vice presidents of sales, and lack of forecasting accuracy impacts many others within the prospective organization.

Table 8.1 Initial Issue-Based Prospecting Script

This is . . .	Gary Walker
with . . .	CustomerCentric Selling.
One of the chief concerns I'm hearing lately from other . . .	senior sales executives
is their frustration with . . .	their inability to produce an accurate revenue forecast resulting in missed revenue goals.

Continued on next page

Continued from previous page

We've been able to help our customers . . .	improve forecasting accuracy.
Can I share a brief story with you explaining how?	

Additionally, this script attempts to appeal to three of the four motivators we introduced previously in Chapter 6, specifically *fear of potential consequences, curiosity about the action of peers,* and *politics within the organization.*

Later, I'll discuss more about the difficulties and effectiveness of telephone prospecting, but for right now I'd like you to develop a simple *issue-based* prospecting script.

Exercise 6. Issue-Based Telephone Prospecting Script

Please refer to the example in Table 8.1 when completing this exercise.

Steps	Script	Your Information
#1. Enter your name in the box at the right.	This is . . .	
#2. Enter the name of the company you work for and represent.	with . . .	

Steps	Script	Your Information
#3. Enter the job title of the senior-level executive you are attempting to engage with. Remember, you can't sell to someone who can't buy. Avoid very specific job titles to avoid mislabeling someone. You don't want to provide anyone with any additional reasons to object to or dismiss your call. I find it safer to go with senior sales executive, senior manufacturing, etc.	One of the chief concerns I'm hearing lately from other . . .	
#4. This step is critical. The issue that you lead with should be a high-probability issue for the job title you are calling. The issue has to be specific to the person if he or she is going to engage.	is their frustration with..	
#5. Enter the goal, problem, or need you specified in step 4 that is being satisfactorily addressed.	We've been able to help our clients . . .	
Can I share a brief story with you explaining how?		

It's only five small pieces of information, but steps 4 and 5 are critical. We are trying to create interest and curiosity with our Sales Ready Messaging. It's about what is important to the prospect and keeping in mind what motivates mainstream prospects.

How to Develop Provocative Messaging

Provocative messaging is about provoking thought as well as seeking a visceral reaction. It is about configuring a product or concept in such a way as to make your prospect do a bit of a double take and think, "Wow!" This means that provocative messaging is about not only thinking creatively but also pushing the envelope regarding what is acceptable.

In the issue-based prospecting script that I introduced earlier, *forecasting accuracy* was the high-probability issue that I used in order to get a senior sales executive to engage with me. Here are three different telephone prospecting scripts that utilize that same high-probability issue:

Script #1. "This is Gary Walker with CustomerCentric Selling. How confident are you that your salespeople will close even 50 percent of what they forecast to close this month? We've been able to help our clients improve forecasting, and I would like to share with you how."

Script #2. "This is Gary Walker with CustomerCentric Selling. Are you under increasing pressure by your executive team to produce monthly revenue forecasts that they can count on? We've been able to help our clients address this issue, and I would like to share with you how."

Script #3. "This is Gary Walker with CustomerCentric Selling. Is missing your revenue forecasts by 50 percent or more, on a monthly basis, acceptable to you and your management team? We've been able to help our clients improve forecasting, and I would like to share with you how."

These three telephone scripts are examples of *provocative messaging*. You will note that all three were developed around the same goal, problem, or need—*forecasting accuracy*. In our particular case, we know that this is one of the top three issues faced by vice presidents of sales.

Each one of the questions posed to the prospect in the telephone prospecting script is meant to be provocative by (1) aligning with a consequence potentially being experienced by the prospect as a result of the sales organization being unable to produce an accurate sales forecast and (2) being very direct, all in your face about the consequence. Remember, *fear of potential consequences* is one of the four things that motivate mainstream prospects.

It's all about the prospect, what the prospect is feeling, experiencing as a result of this issue. Each question is asked in such a way that it is meant to make the prospect feel exposed, vulnerable, and uncomfortable. We are once again trying to create interest and curiosity with this approach. We want to be viewed differently from every other vendor that wants a piece of the prospect's valuable time.

Some additional things to consider when developing your provocative messaging . . .

Provocative Doesn't Mean Being Offensive
Don't allow your message to come across as glib, arrogant, or sarcastic. You are simply attempting to align with what the prospects are thinking but are not willing publicly to admit. You want to grab their attention.

It Is Not About You—It Is About Them
The process of coming up with your powerful, provocative messages—your positioning—doesn't begin with the message itself. *It begins with your prospects*. Who are they? What do they care about and worry about? What other messages are they receiving about people in a line of work similar to yours? And what might you say that will differentiate you and create some interest where none now exists?

Align Your Message
The company or salesperson must conduct sufficient research into the consumer demographic to come up with an original insight about the

prospect's predicament and about how you can help him or her solve a problem or satisfy a goal, problem, or need.

It may simply be a matter of defining the triggering events and crafting a message that resonates and catches the interest of the person who you are seeking to reach. Or it may be based on what you understand to be the high-probability issues of the job title you are seeking to reach that allows you to frame this message in a provocative way, in the vein of being contrarian or of asking the prospect to be contrarian. Remember the irreverent but thoughtful Apple campaign "Think Different" when the company was trying to get users to migrate from the PC several years ago.

Don't Be Afraid to Experiment

Don't be afraid to try new ways of framing the issue or the consequences of not dealing with it. Some issues will be new, and you must be opportunistic. Some issues may be traditional and reoccurring; it is why our companies are successful selling their products and services.

Create a Menu of Goals

You should have a *menu of goals* for each person on your Targeted Conversation List. This menu should change and evolve with the market and with what you are hearing from prospects and clients.

Reference Success Stories

You should have a *success story* that aligns with each of the *goals* on your menu of goals. Following the delivery of our telephone prospecting script, we asked the question, "Can I share a brief story with you explaining how?" Provided the prospect says yes, the approach is to deliver a very brief and scripted story of a situation that is aligned with the issue in the prospecting script. If we were successful in creating interest and curiosity with our approach, a success story is another Sales Ready Messaging tool that we use in the sales process in an attempt to align with our prospect and establish our competency with the aim of continuing the discussion. Our intention is to have prospects listen, relate, and then share something about their situation. Once they do that, the "goal identification" conversation has begun.

There are six components to a success story:

1. *Targeted Conversation List (Industry, Job Title).* Include the job title and industry of an anonymous customer of yours.
2. *Goal.* Identify the goal your anonymous customer had. Success stories for existing offerings are told in the past tense.
3. *Current situation (problem).* Specify the contributing reason preventing the achievement of the goal (addressed by your offering).
4. *Capability (need).* List the capability(ies) that allowed your customer to negate the contributing reason mentioned above.
5. *Benefit statement.* Explain that your company provided this capability. By stating this to your customer, solution ownership remains with the prospect.
6. *Quantified results.* Give measurement (#, $,%) of improvement the customer realized.

Here is an example of a success story that remains aligned with our high-probability issue, *forecasting accuracy,* and is aligned with all the telephone prospecting scripts we have reviewed so far.

Example #1 Success Story

Targeted Conversation (Job Title and Industry)	We recently worked with the VP of sales of a software company. . .
Goal	. . . who wanted to improve forecasting accuracy.
Current Situation (Problem)	Forecasting was difficult because grading was subjective and therefore varied by salesperson. There was no standard way of assessing progress in an opportunity. Additionally, salespeople updated forecasts only when they were required to.

Continued on next page

Continued from previous page

Capability (Need)	The VP wanted to define milestones for the whole company so that, after making calls, salespeople could sign onto a website and be prompted to update opportunities against a standard grading system.
Benefit Statement	CustomerCentric Selling provided him with this capability.
Quantified Results	Over the last six months, forecasting accuracy has risen to 91%. But that's enough about him. Could you tell me about you and your situation?

As you can see, the aim at the conclusion of the success story is to have prospects share something about their situation. Once they do, you will need to be prepared and have the tools to further the conversation toward the desired outcome.

One tool that can really help you is called a Solution Development Prompter (SDP).

Develop an SDP

The key to selling is your ability to converse. You want to have an SDP to facilitate the conversation; diagnose the prospects' goal, problem, or need with bias; and obtain the information you need to document and confirm your understanding of their situation.

An SDP is a Sales Ready Messaging tool that helps salespeople have targeted conversations with prospective buyers. The concept is that if a salesperson can approach a prospecting call with a clear idea of (1) with whom he or she is conversing and (2) where he or she wants the conversation to go, then the chances of success greatly improve.

Picture a traditional salesperson, for example, making a call on a senior sales executive. The executive responds to the salesperson's script and ultimately says, "Our forecasting accuracy has been awful, and this is an area in which I'd like to improve." What would most traditional salespeople do in this situation?

If a traditional salesperson's sales process does not have patience built into it, then that salesperson will attempt to project his or her own solution on the prospect, rather than developing a vision of a solution that the prospect owns. Many sellers launch into something to the effect of "No problem! Let me tell you exactly what you need to improve forecasting accuracy!"

Sharing an opinion or trying to impose that opinion on a prospect won't work in most cases. The natural reaction of the prospect is one of skepticism and pushback. After all, if it were as easy as the salesperson was making it out to be, why has the prospect been struggling with trying to correct it? Instead, once a prospect admits a goal, problem, or need, the salesperson needs two qualities in order to advance the opportunity:

1. A questioning etiquette that provides artificial patience to avoid telling the prospect what he or she needs—imposing the salesperson's opinion
2. Artificial intelligence in the form of questions designed to understand the prospect's current situation, identify what parts of the offering may be needed, and propose what we call "usage scenarios" to the prospect

Why questions? If you are armed with questions, then you are likely to do more asking than telling. Questions precede or facilitate a dialogue or a conversation. This is critical to demonstrate to prospects that you care about their issues and want to obtain a solid understanding of what it is they are dealing with and why. Your ability to converse is your number one selling skill. There is so much more to be learned from your prospects when they are talking and you are listening. Questions by the salesperson encourage the prospect to educate and explain. By asking intelligent questions and having meaningful conversations, you bring value to the interaction. You become more consultative to the prospect, rather than being viewed as a "peddler" of things. Prospects are more comfortable with and more apt to buy from the salesperson who they believe understands their business.

SDPs assist salespeople in having a "contrived conversation" that helps prospects develop "buying visions" that are biased in favor of the salesperson's offering and its capabilities. So having explained that, let me walk you through how SDPs are developed or created.

Step 1. Choose a Job Title and a Goal from the Targeted Conversation List

Choose a job title and corresponding goal from an individual on your Targeted Conversation List. Remember, we developed these in our previous exercise. Each player's goal becomes a conversation that you as a seller should be prepared to have. For the sake of this explanation, our Key Player is the *vice president of sales,* whose goal is to *achieve revenue targets.*

I'll now show you how to begin to build a prompter to facilitate a conversation between you and the job title you have selected and the goal that you have chosen.

Step 2. Identify Features of Your Offering That Support Attainment of the Goal

Traditional product training leads a seller toward wanting to lead with features and functions. This results in a "spray-and-pray" sales call. In an effort to make my point, I have attempted to define CustomerCentric Selling by coming up with a list of features. Look at this list and imagine what would happen if you tried to introduce all these things in a conversation with a senior sales executive.

CustomerCentric Selling Products and Features

1. Prospecting techniques
2. Phone scripts
3. E-mail scripts
4. *Defined sales process*
5. Sales process deliverables
6. *Questioning templates*
7. Success stories

8. Skill practice role plays
9. Sales process control letters
10. *Plausible business emergency*
11. Standardized pipeline milestones
12. Cost-benefit analysis

Leading with features can be deadly when engaging with Key Players. If they engage with a salesperson, they want to focus on what is important to them, their business issues, and ways you can help address those issues. Key Players are not interested in your features, functions, speeds, and feeds.

So our next step in structuring the conversation is to identify *only* those features that can be used to achieve the prospects' stated goal. We are making a conscious decision to limit our features. As you can see in the list above, I've highlighted in italics the four most relevant features that would help the vice president of sales attain his or her goal of achieving revenue targets: defined sales process, questioning templates, plausible business emergency, and cost-benefit analysis.

Step 3. Convert Features into Usage Scenarios

If a salesperson simply blurted out "defined sales process" to a vice president of sales, that wouldn't be meaningful and the prospect wouldn't understand why a defined sales process is even relevant. The phrase would mean much more to me than to the buyer. *Feature names* (nouns) don't help prospects understand how features *can* or *could be used* (verbs). Think about what happens when people go into the hardware store. They are not purchasing a ½-inch drill bit; they are purchasing a ½-inch hole. They are purchasing what it does, not what it is. Therefore an additional step is needed to convert features into usage scenarios.

Usage scenarios have four components:

Event: The circumstance causing a need for the specific feature.
Question: A situational question that refers to the event.
Player: Who (or what) will take action to respond to the event.

Action: How the feature can be used, stated in terms that the buyers can understand and relate to their job title. The description of the action should be specific enough so that buyers can visualize how the event will be addressed.

Let's take a closer look at the feature "defined sales process" to create a usage scenario for a conversation with a vice president of sales about the goal of achieving revenue targets:

Event: When engaging with a prospect
Question: would your salespeople be more effective sellers if . . .
Player: the sales organization
Action: utilized a consistent, repeatable sales process (1) that it can be taught to execute, (2) that you can monitor, coach, and inspect, and (3) that represents your most effective sales practices

Please note that the degree of specificity in the action is deliberate. If it simply read "used a process," instead of "utilized a consistent, repeatable sales process," the vice president of sales would have no way of understanding how that would be accomplished.

Here are the other three features from the list above that I selected for my discussion with the vice president of sales about achieving revenue targets that have been converted into the usage-scenario format:

Event: When meeting with a senior executive
Question: could the converse more effectively if . . .
Player: your salespeople
Action: had questioning templates that combine application and product-usage knowledge, by job title, that allow them to converse and diagnose an executive's business issues with a bias toward your product's capabilities

Event: When involved in a competitive sales situation
Question: could you win more opportunities if . . .
Player: your salespeople

Action: knew how to introduce and exploit features and capabilities, unique to your offerings, to differentiate [company name] from its competitors and potentially set traps from which they are unable to recover

Event: When competing for limited funds or budget
Question: would they be more successful if . . .
Player: your salespeople
Action: had the ability to measure the cost of how business is being done today and calculate the potential value to the prospect's organization in order to add additional logic in support of the purchase decisions, obtain management consensus, and eliminate the "no decisions" that you have experienced

What we have done is to develop usage scenarios in the event, question, player, action (EQPA) format for *defined sales process, questioning templates, plausible business emergency,* and *cost-benefit analysis.*

Step 4. Document Diagnostic Questions

In the same way that sellers shouldn't lead with features, I don't want to lead with usage scenarios. Therefore, the next step is to create a corresponding set of diagnostic questions for the salesperson to ask in order to determine if the buyer has a need for the usage scenario described in the EQPA question. These questions are not meant to represent the complete conversation. What we are doing here is creating a Solution Development Prompter, with *prompter* being the operative word. The questions are used to facilitate a diagnostic conversation between the seller and the prospect and to ultimately diagnose the prospect's goal, problem, or need with bias toward what you sell. In addition, it is helpful to provide questions that can be used to explore and measure what it is costing the prospect to operate without your capabilities, so that you can begin to calculate the potential value of the usage scenario to your prospect.

Diagnostic questions are used to obtain a better understanding of how the prospect is operating today—e.g., achieve revenue targets—

and, ideally, what it currently costs the prospect to operate that way. At the same time, good diagnostic questions help you to establish your competency, in the same way a physician meeting you for the first time builds credibility by asking insightful, intelligent questions that you are capable of answering.

Table 8.2 is a completed SDP that includes all the diagnostic questions in the column on the left-hand side. Each set of questions is aligned with a specific usage scenario. These are all questions that a competent salesperson should be capable of asking a buyer. The question set for diagnosing the first issue, "no defined sales process," is purposely broad and benign—to invite the prospect to provide an overview, to explain. Each subsequent question allows the salesperson to peel back the prospect's original explanation, with the goal of uncovering potential sales process issues that are contributing reasons to this executive not meeting his or her revenue targets. These can be addressed by the seller's usage scenarios. This approach is what I have referred to as *diagnosis with bias*.

So we now have completed an SDP. Additional SDPs should be created for each remaining goal contained in the menu of goals for the vice president of sales. After that, this same process would be repeated for each job title and menu item that is specific to your vertical markets and offerings. The final result is Sales Ready Messaging tools that enable you to confidently and knowledgeably converse with the senior executives that you have identified as being the people to engage with in order to sell, fund, and implement your product or service.

Leverage Other Collateral
What other collateral or electronic "leave-behinds" do you have? These could include white papers, brochures, e-newsletters, etc.

Organize the Information
Gather it up. Organize it. Store it where you can find it quickly. Refresh it. It is one of the keys to your prospecting and business development effectiveness.

Table 8.2 SDP

Title: VP of Sales   ***Goal:*** Achieve Revenue Targets   ***Offering:*** CustomerCentric Selling

"What barriers to achieving revenue targets exist today?"   "What capabilities are you looking for to help you achieve your revenue targets?"

Issue #1. No defined sales process	
• Could you provide me an overview of your current sales process?	*Event:* When engaging with a prospect,
• Do salespeople tend to rely on their "own process," rather than what you just described?	*Question:* would your salespeople be more effective sellers if . . .
• Has lack of "sales process" created performance issues?	*Player:* the sales organization
• Does this create coaching challenges?	*Action:* had a consistent, repeatable sales process (1) that it can be taught to execute, (2) that you can monitor, coach and inspect, and (3) that represents your most effective or best sales practices?
Issue #2. Difficulty conversing with decision makers	
• Whom do your salespeople typically sell to?	*Event:* When meeting with a senior executive
• Do they have difficulty gaining access to and remaining at the executive level?	*Question:* could they converse more effectively if . . .
• How fluent are they in discussing business issues with executives?	*Player:* your salespeople
• Do you waste time trying to sell to the wrong people?	*Action:* had sales tools or questioning templates that combine application and product-usage knowledge, by job
• Are sale cycles too long? What should they be?	title, that allow them to converse and diagnose an executive's business issues with a bias toward your product's capabilities?

Continued on next page

"What barriers to achieving revenue targets exist today?"

"What capabilities are you looking for to help you achieve your revenue targets?"

Issue #3. Don't leverage competitive differentiators • Do you have product or service attributes that are unique to your product or service? • Has anyone made a list of what they are and how to position them against named competitors? Do salespeople know what they are and how to position them effectively? • Can you identify an opportunity where you lost to an inferior product or service?	*Event:* When involved in a competitive sales situation *Question:* could you win more opportunities if. . . *Player:* your salespeople *Action:* knew how to introduce and exploit features and capabilities, unique to your offerings, to differentiate [company name] from competitors and potentially set traps from which your competitor is unable to recover?
Issue #4. Difficulty documenting value • Do proposals include the total cost of ownership or just your cost? • Whose numbers do your salespeople use—theirs or the prospect's? • Do proposals include a value justification (cost-benefit analysis)? • Are your salespeople dependent upon the prospect determining the value and total cost of ownership of your proposals?	*Event:* When competing for limited funds or budget *Question:* would it help if . . . . *Player:* your salespeople *Action:* had the ability to measure the cost of how business is being done today and calculate the potential value to the prospect's organization in order to add additional logic in support of the purchase decisions?
Recap: "So the way you do it today is . . . ? Did I understand you correctly?"	*Confirm solution:* "If you had [capabilities], could you achieve [goal]?"

Exercise 7. Creating an SDP

Using the steps outlined, use the blank table provided below to create your own sample SDP.

Title: *Goal:*   *Offering:*

"What barriers to achieving [goal] exist today?"

"What capabilities are you looking for to help you achieve your [goal]?"

Issue #1.	*Event:*
	Question:
	Player:
	Action:
Issue #2.	*Event:*
	Question:
	Player:
	Action:

Continued on next page

Continued from previous page

"What barriers to achieving [goal] exist today?"

"What capabilities are you looking for to help you achieve your [goal]?"

Issue #3.	*Event:*
	Question:
	Player:
	Action:
Issue #4.	*Event:*
	Question:
	Player:
	Action:
Recap: "So the way you do it today is . . . ? Did I understand you correctly?"	*Confirm solution:* "If you had [capabilities], could you achieve [goal]?"

When we began this chapter, I stated that the purpose of the chapter was to *introduce* you to the Sales Ready Messaging tools that we believe should be developed for sales teams to use. The SDP that I introduced in this chapter is not needed for prospecting and business development; however, once a prospect has agreed to engage with you as a result of your prospecting activities, you need to be prepared to converse effectively.

If properly prepared, Sales Ready Messaging tools will provide for a more consistent positioning of your offering, enhance your situational expertise, give you the courage and confidence to engage in meaningful conversation with your prospect, and improve your overall sales efforts.

A few other thoughts about sales messaging:

1. Marketing should take responsibility for creating and maintaining the Sales Ready Messaging tools, with significant involvement from the sales organization. Marketing typically is responsible for how the company's product and services will be described and positioned in the market. Additionally, marketing often communicates with the customer after implementation to gather information about the client's satisfaction and product use to author success stories. This information can prove to be invaluable. You don't need two organizations describing different variations of what your products and services are and what they do. Marketing, with significant ongoing involvement from the sales organization, is the way.

2. SDPs should be reviewed on a monthly basis to ensure they remain relevant to the marketplace and reflect what the sales organization is hearing from its prospects. This requires the creation and execution of a formal closed-loop feedback system.

3. A single SDP may represent the integration of multiple products and services.

4. SDPs become easier to develop after you have developed the first one.

5. You'll find usage scenarios can be multipurposed or wordsmithed to address multiple individuals and conversations.

6. SDPs represent a *contrived conversation*. They should be biased toward your offering's capabilities. You want people to buy what you sell!

7. Sales Ready Messaging should be part of any new product or service release. Don't squander any competitive advantage your new offering may provide. Instead of salespeople having to take months to figure out how to position their new offering, it should be figured out for them in advance.

Checkpoint #15

	True	False
1. If you can't converse effectively with your prospect, you will be outsold by the vendor who can.		
2. The purpose of sales ready messaging is to equip the salesperson to converse about the prospect's goals, problems, and needs.		
3. Companies should prepare their salespeople to converse with prospects about their offerings by developing tools that salespeople can use.		
4. Scripts allow us to determine what works and what doesn't work.		
5. Scripts that are found to be ineffective should be changed.		
6. The goal of provocative messaging is to provoke interest without being offensive or arrogant.		
7. Success stories are used to establish your competency and encourage the prospect to share a goal, problem, or need.		
8. An SDP helps salespeople have conversations with prospective buyers.		
9. Questions by the salesperson encourage the prospect to educate and explain.		
10. Sales Ready Messaging provides for more consistent positioning of your offering by the sales organization.		
11. Salespeople do a better job positioning their offerings when they make it up on the fly.		

	True	False
12. The SDP represents the complete and total conversation a salesperson should have with a prospect.		
13. Prospects don't care about whom you've worked with and what they have accomplished.		
14. Success stories are just that—stories, fables.		
15. Sales Ready Messaging tools are a waste of time.		

Answers: 1–10 are true; 11–15 are false.

Chapter 9

LEVERAGING RELATIONSHIPS AND RESULTS THROUGH SOCIAL NETWORKING

Social Networking

In the Introduction to this book, I made reference to the *Selling to Senior Executives* study (*Kenan-Flagler Business School, University of North Carolina*). This study revealed that decision makers and senior executives are *much* more likely to meet with salespeople who were referred by someone either inside or outside the company. I'm going to share the aggregated responses with you. These executives indicated that 84 percent of the time they would engage with a salesperson if it was as a result of a referral. It doesn't take a genius to conclude that obtaining referrals might be good for prospecting and business development efforts! But what if you don't know anyone at a company you would like to do business with—what then?

Building and maintaining a professional network takes time. Think of this as an example. Maybe you've found yourself in this situation in your career. Unexpectedly, you have just lost your job and you need to find a new one. You immediately begin to prepare a list of people whom you can reach out to for help. Even though you would like your list to be long, you find it's quite short. As you begin reviewing the names on your list, you also begin to think, "When was the last time that I spoke with this person?" You quickly conclude that not only is the list short, but you haven't been particularly good at remaining in contact with most of the people on your list. You further conclude that in pursuit of your job and your other activities, you have neglected your network and sometimes even friendships.

If you have neglected building and maintaining your network for years, you can't expect to build a strong, productive network overnight. But you *can* get started overnight. Here are some ways how . . .

A Word About Social Networking

Many of us belong to one or more social networks; then again, some of us resist the invitation to join. After all, with everything going on in your business life, how can you keep up with all your social networks? Not only that, but some employers see their employees' participation in any social network as a productivity drain. I think before we begin to talk about what social networking is and how we can use social networking to become more effective prospectors, it's important to gain a global perspective.

How Big Is Social Networking?

Here are some snapshot statistics:

Social Networking (2011)

- 47 percent of online adults use social networking sites.
- 73 percent of teens and young adults are members of at least one social network.

Facebook

- More than 1.5 million local businesses have active pages on Facebook.

- The average user spends more than 55 minutes per day on Facebook.
- Facebook has 400 million-plus active users, with over 1.5 million business pages.

Twitter

- Twitter has 24 million-plus unique visitors per month, with 500 million tweets per day.
- 11 percent (or 33.88 million) of U.S. online adults use Twitter.
- There are approximately 50 million tweets sent per day, at about 600 tweets per second.

LinkedIn

- LinkedIn has 161 million-plus professionals worldwide, including all Fortune 500 companies.
- Professionals are joining at the rate of 2 per second.
- The global average time spent per person on social networking sites is now nearly 5½ hours per month.
- The active U.S.-based social network audience grew roughly 9 percent from 149 million in February 2010 to 161 million in March 2012.

Unique Visitors per Month

Facebook: 1,136,644,000
MySpace: 17,935,000
Twitter: 10,789,000
LinkedIn: 17,020,000

What Is Social Networking?

A social networking service is an online service, platform, or site that focuses on building and reflecting social networks or social relations among people who share interests and activities. A social network service essentially consists of a representation of each user (often a profile), his or her social links, and a variety of additional services. Most social network services are web based and provide means of communication, such as e-mail and instant messaging, that participants can use to interact over the Internet; online community services are sometimes considered a social network service, though in a broader sense, a social network service usually means an individual-centered service.

How Is It Used in Business?

Social networking sites allow users to connect with other individuals within the network, monitor activities of site members, share ideas and expertise, promote activities and events, request assistance, seek expertise, and communicate within their individual networks.

What's in It for Me?

Through social networking, you can:

- Expand your influence and connect with new people with similar interests
- Connect and communicate with your existing customers
- Leverage your relationships and results
- Engage in the ongoing dialogue
- Contribute your expertise and become a "go-to" person and a resource
- Promote yourself
- Promote your company
- Research potential prospect organizations
- Find Key Players
- Ask for and obtain referrals to Key Players
- Connect and communicate with the Key Players of prospect organizations
- Monitor activities and think *triggering events*
- Participate in special interest groups

Using LinkedIn

LinkedIn is just one of the many social networking sites that people belong to. I don't know of anyone in sales who isn't aware of its existence. Some people fondly refer to it as "Facebook with a tie." As of February 2012, LinkedIn reported that it had more than 161 million-plus worldwide members, and people were signing up to become members at the rate of *two people every second.*

Now having said that, I know there are still salespeople who don't belong to LinkedIn. How do I know? Every time I conduct a workshop, I invite my students to join our CustomerCentric Selling special interest group on LinkedIn. When I look at the list of invitees, I can see who belongs and who doesn't; those who belong to LinkedIn have e-mail addresses that are displayed in blue, and those who are not members have black e-mail addresses. There are tons of you who still haven't joined. What are you waiting for?

Let me be direct. If you are a sales professional and do not belong to LinkedIn, go to http://www.linkedin.com and sign up now. Belonging to LinkedIn and using all its capabilities can allow you to rapidly grow your professional network and aid in your prospecting and business development efforts.

LinkedIn Business Development Checklist

After signing up for your account, the next thing you are going to need to do is fill out your profile. You want to make it as professional and complete as possible. You'll find that there are online firms that specialize in helping individuals to develop their profiles based on what they are trying to accomplish. For example, salespeople who are looking for work would have different profiles from salespeople who are gainfully employed and wanting to be viewed as a resource and expert in the market that they sell into. This is your online brochure. All the people on LinkedIn are working to put their best foot forward. I've created this checklist to help get you started.

1. Manage your professional identity—create a LinkedIn profile.
   - Go to http://www.linkedin.com and fill in the blanks under "Join LinkedIn" today. Fill the form out entirely, including all relevant content to your business and expertise.
   - Add key words that you want your clients and prospects to find you by. Align your profile to match your target market.

- Your Public Profile LinkedIn address should be your name, e.g., http://www.linkiedin.com/in/[your name].
- In "Additional Information," add links to your blogs and website.
- Under "Privacy Settings," make your profile as public as possible.
- Under "Network Updates," list any webinars, podcasts, seminars, tradeshows you will be attending or conducting, etc.
- Include a color photo (this can be uploaded from your own camera or a digital photo studio).
- LinkedIn is free; however, I recommend upgrading to a business account. It provides you with the ability to request more introductions, use LinkedIn's InMail capability, etc. The site has a section that contrasts the different plans, capabilities, and costs.
- Key point: When you prospect, it is very likely the prospects will look at your profile before deciding to engage with you. Make it an easy decision for them.

2. Build and engage with your professional network.
   - This is a professional network. This is not a place where you reconnect and communicate with friends and family members. Use Facebook, MySpace, etc., for that.
   - The size of *your* network will determine the success of your networking and referral efforts.
   - Send requests to connect with other people—clients, coworkers, prospects, etc.
   - Add people who give you their business card, if they can be a source of new business or referrals.
   - Use LinkedIn to sift through your Outlook, Yahoo, and other contacts and send people who are relevant to your efforts an invitation to connect.
   - Accept invitations to connect from people you know or have met.
   - Add your LinkedIn web address to the signature line on e-mail. LinkedIn provides you with that capability.

3. Get active and develop your professional reputation—this *is* about you!
   - Contact clients, former managers, and coworkers and request that they write a recommendation for you *if* it is relevant to your existing sales role and what you are trying to accomplish. Within "Your Profile," there is a "Request Recommendations" link.
4. Identify special interest groups who may be predisposed to your message.
   - Search "Groups" to find industries, associations, and special interest groups that your clients belong to and *join!*
5. Contribute, contribute, contribute.
   - Start a "Discussion" within the group (and become viewed as a leader and resource). Pick events and issues your clients face, issues you want to become known for helping companies address.
6. Read LinkedIn News—monitor what is going on and look for triggering events that you could use.
   - Monitor the daily posts you get from LinkedIn that highlight the changes in the lives of your contacts.
   - Be on alert for people who have started or left jobs, because they can be a source of business. Even if people have merely changed their "experience," investigate and find out what has really changed.
   - Be outgoing. Ask to set up a brief telephone call or host a LinkedIn Meetup in your city or at a conference.
7. Check to see who has viewed your profile.
   - People who are viewing your profile may be interested in your offering, need help, etc. Reach out to them. Consider making them part of your prospecting efforts.
8. Use the "Advanced People Search" capability.
   - In the upper right-hand corner is an "Advanced" selection. Use this to build a list of individual prospects by job title and name.
9. Take advantage of the "Request an Introduction" capability.

- *Key point: Referrals are the number one reason senior executives cite for agreeing to speak with a salesperson.*
- Request introductions from people in your network, preferably first-degree connections.
- Use the Request an Introduction capability to get introduced to people you may have identified in item 9, above.
- Be professional with your approach if you expect to obtain the introduction you are seeking.

As I have noted, LinkedIn can be used as a terrific tool for rapidly developing your network and individual relationships in a systematic fashion. However, technology platforms have a tendency to come and go, and since I have no way of knowing when you are reading and applying the lessons of this book, you may need to explore other alternatives as they become available—and as others disappear. Such is the fate of any business based on information technology. New entrants are emerging all the time.

Regardless of whether LinkedIn is your tool of choice, the approach outlined for developing a strong network that can provide the access you need to executives is crucial and can work with numerous systems. After all, in the early days it was simply done with paper and a Rolodex, so place the greatest emphasis on *why* to do it, rather than *how* to do it.

Exercise 8. Requesting Introductions via LinkedIn

Let's try this exercise to practice how you could request introductions via LinkedIn.

1. From the company you identified in Exercise 4 (in Chapter 6), select an individual by name who you would like to communicate with. Enter the individual's name and job title below.
   Name: _____
   Job Title: _____
2. Find that person within LinkedIn.

- You can perform a simple name search, or if that is unsuccessful, you may want to use the "Advanced Search" capability at the top of the page.

3. On the individual's Profile Page, locate the "How you are connected to . . ." information box on the right-hand side of the page.
    - Look to see if you have any first-degree connections. If you do, proceed to step 4.
4. From the top right-hand quadrant of the page, select "Get introduced through a connection."
5. Select from the list of "shared connections" presented the individual you would like to provide you with the introduction, and select "continue."
6. Complete the "Request Introduction" screen.
    - Make sure your message to your prospect is not too "salesy" . . . create curiosity and interest.
    - Present your message as an opportunity to speak with your prospect about something you know to be an issue (triggering event) or you assume to be an issue based on research, market conditions, etc.
    - Write a brief note to your LinkedIn contact who you are asking to provide the introduction.

Checkpoint #16

Have you created a profile on LinkedIn yet?	
Where can you look on LinkedIn for triggering events?	
What is the number one reason senior executives agree to speak with a salesperson?	

Chapter *10*

PROSPECTING METHODS

If you are new to sales or even if you are an experienced salesperson, chances are that you are not too fond of prospecting for new business. Wait—that's too kind—you *despise* prospecting.

That is understandable because, quite frankly, prospecting is an activity that most salespeople and their sponsoring organizations as a whole do exactly the wrong way. They focus on closing and servicing accounts, taking for granted that "anyone can prospect" and that prospecting is somehow as fundamental as breathing. The fact of the matter is that it is not that easy—but it is vital. As I've stated earlier, prospecting and business development lead to selling.

Unfortunately, up until now there has been little or no training offered to salespeople to help them improve their prospecting skills. Sure, there are a lot of companies that offer "cold-calling" classes, but prospecting and business development are more than just cold calling.

In 1995, Target Marketing Systems and Hewlett Packard Corporation, in conjunction with the Kenan-Flagler Business School at the University of North Carolina, undertook a research study to identify and understand what factors help professional salespeople establish trust and credibility with senior executives and why senior executives grant continued access to some salespeople while denying access to others. The results of that study were published in a white paper entitled *Selling to Senior Executives—How Salespeople Establish Trust and Credibility with Senior Executives*.

The purpose of this book is not to recount the entire study. However, there is a portion of it that is very insightful and lends credibility to the information, methods, and tactics that I'm sharing with you in this book.

The researchers asked the respondents what was the most effective means for a salesperson to reach or gain an audience with them. The results of the response to that question are given in Table 10.1.

Table 10.1 Effectiveness of Methods Used to Gain a Meeting with Senior Executives

	Always	Usually	Occasionally	Never
A recommendation from someone inside your company	16%	68%	16%	0%
A referral from outside the company	8%	36%	44%	12%
A letter from a salesperson followed by a direct call	4%	20%	40%	36%
A contact at an off-site meeting	0%	44%	32%	24%
A direct telephone call from a salesperson	0%	20%	36%	44%

Information from *Selling to Senior Executives—How Salespeople Establish Trust and Credibility with Senior Executives*, Kenan-Flagler Business School, University of North Carolina.

Effectiveness of Methods Used to Gain a Meeting with Senior Executives

Of all the methods used by salespeople to gain an audience with senior executives, the *study participants ranked all but one as relatively ineffective*. Cold calls were least successful.

Of all the study participants, 80 percent said they would *never* or only *occasionally* grant an interview to salespeople making cold calls. Nor is a letter sent before a call likely to improve the chances of obtaining the desired meeting.

Slightly more than half the executives interviewed preferred not to be introduced to salespeople through referrals from people outside the executive's organization, whereas almost half said that they would agree to a meeting through a referral outside the company. It's almost a toss-up.

By far the most effective means of getting a meeting with a senior executive is a recommendation from someone within the executive's own company. *Eighty-four percent of the respondents indicated they would usually or always grant a meeting to a salesperson based on an introduction or recommendation from inside the company.*

Think back to the previous chapter where we discussed LinkedIn, where we stressed the importance of developing and maintaining your network and utilizing the automated introduction capability within LinkedIn to obtain those all-important referrals. LinkedIn has automated for you the most effective method for obtaining access to the people you want to sell to!

In keeping with our need to become and remain customer-centric, I'm suggesting that we use this research and analysis to guide the development of our prospecting and business development plan and our behavior.

Before we get into some specific methods and accompanying tactics on how to make you a more successful prospector and, as a result, a more successful and wealthier salesperson, let me offer you this thought. If prospecting is so universally loathed, does this not create an opportunity for you to develop a tremendous and sustainable advantage over your peers and competitors? Try not to follow the herd of salespeople who cringe at the thought of prospecting. Instead, endeavor to be the lone wolf who embraces it, perfects it, and uses it as a catalyst to drive ongoing sales.

Now let us discuss how to do just that.

In the following chapters I would like to share with you:

- The different prospecting methods
- Where applicable, the pros and cons of each
- The relative effectiveness of each method
- Nuances to each approach
- Examples of how, individually, the methods might be used
- Ways they may be used tactically, in parallel, to enhance their overall effectiveness
- Examples of each method

Which Prospecting Method Should I Use?

There are seven key methods you can use to engage with your prospects, and some of these methods can be combined or used in series to enhance your prospecting effectiveness:

1. Telephone
2. E-mail
3. Telephone and e-mail—"thunder and lightning"
4. Direct mail
5. Social networking
6. Referrals
7. Drip nurturing

We have already addressed one of the methods—social networking—in Chapter 9. We'll focus on the remaining methods in subsequent chapters.

Checkpoint #17

Of all the prospecting methods, which one has been found to be the least successful?	
What is the most effective means of getting a senior executive to meet with you?	

What percentage of senior executives will accept a call from a salesperson?	
What are some of the various methods of prospecting that you can use to develop new business?	

Chapter *11*

TELEPHONE PROSPECTING

"Typical" Telephone Prospecting

When salespeople and the companies they work for think about *prospecting*, they think about cold-call telephone prospecting. It's the de facto standard and has been for years. Think about the sales training programs you've attended. If they contained a prospecting component, it was probably a discussion and practice around cold calling. We still cover it in our CustomerCentric Selling and Prospecting and Business Development Workshops, and we are going to talk about it here.

Some companies assign their salespeople a specific number of outbound cold calls that they have to make each day. It's part of their daily performance standards or criteria. Unfortunately, monitoring the number of calls made may not be particularly relevant or effective. Anyone should be able to pick up the telephone and make an outbound call. However, I think there are a number of other things I would prefer to monitor. For instance, whom (job title) did they call, were they able to get the person on the telephone, did they reach an administrative assistant, did they reach voice mail, and did the individual engage based on the goal, problem, or need that was the focus of the script. I need qualitative information to know what's working and what's not. I can use that information to become more effective. In the end I would prefer a single call where the prospect engaged with the salesperson rather than learning that the salesperson made 10 outbound dials. The emphasis should be on the *quality* of the telephone prospecting effort, not just the quantity.

Picture this for a moment. While you are reading this book, your telephone begins to ring. You look at your caller ID, and not recognizing the name or number, you allow the call to go to voice mail. You'll check it when you can. You have just enlisted your caller ID and voice mail to become your screener of unwanted calls.

Let's say that when you finish reading this chapter, your curiosity gets the best of you. You put down this book and pick up your telephone to listen to your voice messages. As you listen, if it's someone you don't know or someone who is trying to sell you something (a cold call), you delete the message. Is this not what happens? Well, your prospects are doing the same thing to you.

In doing research for this book and developing our Prospecting and Business Development Workshop, I came across a statistic attributed to ConnectAndSell, a live-conversation automation company. The statistic was that it takes 21 dials to make a single connection. That means that it took 21 dials for the salesperson to connect with the prospect. However, ConnectAndSell didn't report what happened once the parties were connected, whether the salesperson had a conversation, was hung up on, etc. In any case, a 21-to-1 ratio is a 4.7 percent conversion rate. I'm not sure many companies want their high-priced sales talent smiling and dialing with a conversion rate like that! Suffice it to say, ConnectAndSell recognized this and seems to have developed a very nice business.

As we learned from the Kenan-Flagler study, cold calling is the *least effective means* of gaining access to a senior executive. Some senior executives hate receiving cold calls from salespeople almost as much as salespeople hate making them! Nevertheless, cold calling remains a commonly used method, and it is worthy of discussion.

We also know from the Kenan-Flagler study that while cold calling is the least effective means, 20 percent of the senior executives surveyed indicated that "usually" they will accept a call from a salesperson. So the question becomes this: is it the method or how the method is used by salespeople that renders it minimally effective. I believe it is a combination of both.

Here are some of my observations about why it has become minimally effective. As you read them, just for fun, place a check mark next to those that you agree with:

☐ Salespeople dislike making cold calls.
☐ Prospects dislike receiving cold calls.
☐ Most salespeople have not been trained on how to cold-call.
☐ Cold calling is typically undertaken in response to a weak pipeline.
☐ It's hard work.
☐ Salespeople are unprepared . . . no plan . . . they wing it.
☐ They use a one-size-fits-all approach. The scripts are generic regardless of job title or industry.
☐ It's all about the salespeople: they lead with the products.
☐ They call people too low in the organization to buy what they sell.
☐ Salespeople lead with ineffective questions:
  • "How are you today?"
  • "Is now a good time?"
  • "Do you have a minute?"
  • "Are you looking to buy . . .?"
☐ Salespeople do most of the talking.
☐ Salespeople become frustrated with the lack of success and give up quickly.
☐ Salespeople conclude that cold calling simply doesn't work.

What do you think? How many check marks did you make? Are these some of the same things you've observed or experienced? Are these some of the same reasons why you are not as effective as you'd like to be? In this chapter I will share with you some approaches and techniques that you can add to your prospecting tool set.

CustomerCentric Telephone Prospecting

Let's take a look at telephone prospecting through a CustomerCentric Selling lens. Imagine you are sitting at your desk and the phone rings. You look at the caller ID, don't recognize the number, but answer it anyway. This is what you hear:

> This is John Smith with ABC sales training. How are you today? (brief pause) We take great pride in our outstanding reputation for sales training. We offer multiple training courses in sales and sales management and would welcome the opportunity to spend 30 minutes with you to discuss your training requirements. Is now a good time, or would you like to schedule some time to speak later this afternoon?

Makes you wish you didn't pick up the phone, doesn't it? While everything that was said may be true, there are several things that prospects might find objectionable in this approach, all of which reduce this salesperson's likelihood of getting this prospect to engage. For example:

- The script contains an insincere personal question in the second sentence. The salesperson is trying to sell you something—does he or she really care how you are?
- Next, a biased opinion of sales training is offered. Doesn't every sales training company say its training is the best?
- The script mentions a specific product or service: training courses in sales and sales management. What are the chances you were thinking about a goal, problem, or need related to sales or sales management training that you were trying to address? Assuming that you don't hang up, you will probably want to know about cost. It would be virtually impossible to provide a meaningful response, given variables such as sales issues that need to be addressed, number of salespeople, average transaction size, salesperson quotas, etc.
- The script is presumptive; it puts pressure on the prospect for a conversation right now or later the same day. As I pointed out

earlier in the book, the prospect might agree to a later appointment simply to get you off the phone, reject your invite for the appointment, and never accept a call from you again.

The objective of any script is getting the person that you are trying to reach to *engage* with you . . . to begin a dialogue. You are not going to sell anyone anything with this phone call, and an appointment may be totally inappropriate until you both mutually agree that there is something worth discussing further.

We suggest that your script can be far more effective if you attempt to align it with what *you believe or know* to be affecting the person you are calling. Is it possible that there is some vice president of sales sitting at a desk dealing with a myriad of sales performance issues and thinking about how he or she is going to address them? Probably. But in almost every case, there is very little upside to leading with your product (sales and sales management training).

In Exercise 4 (in Chapter 6), you identified those high-probability issues that you *believed* a particular job title would be interested in. These were based on you and your company's experience and knowledge of your market.

In Exercise 5 (in Chapter 7), you identified triggering events—events that, if they happen to an organization or individual you have targeted, will create an immediate opportunity for you to engage.

Here are two different scripts, one is a basic telephone prospecting script based on what you believe—*market knowledge*; the second script is based on what you know to have occurred—*a triggering event*. Both can be delivered in about 15 seconds or less.

Telephone Script #1. What You Believe (Market Knowledge)

This is Gary Walker with CustomerCentric Selling. One of the chief concerns that we have been hearing from other senior sales executives is their inability to produce an accurate forecast resulting in missed revenue targets. We've been able to help our clients improve forecasting accuracy, and I'd like an opportunity to share with you how.

Telephone Script #2. What You Know (Triggering Event)

This is Gary Walker with CustomerCentric Selling. I saw on BusinessWire that your stock price was adversely impacted due to your inability to deliver on third-quarter forecasted revenues. We've been able to help our clients improve forecasting accuracy, and I'd like an opportunity to share with you how.

Note that in both scripts we've eliminated the personal question and our opinion about sales training. Rather than mention sales and sales management training, we've led with an issue that we believe, or know, that this job title, this individual, has to deal with. The scripts simply ask if you are interested in how we helped somebody in your same job, with your same job title, deal effectively with a problem we believe or know you have. The scripts head off the premature discussion on price and end in a way that makes a yes-no response difficult.

Dealing with Common Responses

We believe that if the script results in the prospect engaging with the salesperson, it was successful. So let's discuss the most common responses you are most likely to get and how to handle them. Keep in mind that you cannot begin to sell until a buyer shares a goal or admits a problem that you can help him or her to address—"no goal, no prospect." Here are some potential responses:

1. *The prospect shows no interest.* "Not a problem for me" or "I'm not interested."

It could be the person is busy, is in a bad mood because you just intruded on his or her workday, is presently not focused on the business issue you lead with, or legitimately doesn't have this business issue you lead with. The most important thing to remember in this situation is not to take the lack of interest or rejection personally. It's not about you!

When you get this response, you have to have a place to branch to or this is going to be a short call. We suggest that you offer the other menu of goal items that you identified. You can make that transition by saying:

Other issues that senior sales executives have asked us to help them address include:

- Lengthy time from new hire to first sale
- Wasting resources on unqualified opportunities
- 13 percent of the sales team carrying the entire group

Would you like to learn how we've helped our customers address any of these issues?

This yes-no question answers in one of two ways. Either the buyer is curious about one or more of these items, in which case you can have a conversation, or the buyer expresses no interest. In the latter case, thank the person for his or her time and close professionally. Send an e-mail documenting and confirming what you had inquired about, and invite the person to reconnect with you should he or she begin to experience any of those issues.

Keep in mind that prospecting should be done at several levels in the same organization. Even if one or more people you contacted were not interested, referring to our previous exercises, you still have other people with different goals that will allow you to pursue the account.

Later in this chapter, when we talk about organizing to telephone-prospect, we describe how we use the results of our exercises to plan our transition.

Now that we've discussed response #1—the prospect shows no interest—let's turn our attention to two other possible responses:

2. *The buyer shows immediate interest in an issue from the menu.*
3. The buyer expresses passive interest and asks you to send some information.

Response #2 is what you want to hear. You simply continue the conversation focusing on that issue.

Response #3, however, is another matter. Inexperienced salespeople see this response as a positive sign. More experienced salespeople are more cynical and for good reason. They believe this to be a convenient and polite way for prospects to get salespeople to leave them alone. When it comes time to follow up, the prospects won't take your call, or the administrative assistant will tell you that the information has been received and that they will contact you if they are interested. It's a classic "don't call us, we'll call you."

When you get a request to send information in lieu of having a conversation, do both you and the prospect a favor by indicating that due to your extensive offering, you wouldn't know what to send. Rather than send information that is not applicable to what the prospect is trying to accomplish, invite the person to spend 15 minutes with you on the telephone educating you so that you can make an informed selection about what to send.

Organizing to Prospect

I shudder to think at the number of times I have seen a salesperson pick up the phone and dial to prospect with little or no preparation. The results are predictable, and the salesperson follows the herd's thinking that prospecting does not work, is too hard, and is too much work.

I suspect you can see how foolish that approach sounds, and it is strange to imagine why any salesperson would not want to fully prepare for that all-important first impression—the conversation that will lead instantly to failure or ultimately to a carefully managed, mutually beneficial business transaction. By reading this book, you are showing an interest in prospecting the "right" way, and the right way begins with being organized for success.

To begin, you must assume that every time you dial the phone, you *will* make contact (the person you are attempting to reach, the person's administrative assistant, or the person's voice mail). Expect it. Believe it. Then prepare for it by (1) creating interest and curiosity with your approach and (2) remaining in alignment with the person to whom you are speaking by using:

- A carefully prepared, 12- to 15-second script
- A menu of goals, problems, and needs
- Corresponding success stories

Here's an example of what I mean by being organized to prospect:

Targeted Job Title: **Sales Executive, Information Technology Company**

This is Gary Walker with CustomerCentric Selling. One of the primary concerns I hear from other senior sales executives is their frustration with missed revenue targets due to inaccurate forecasts by salespeople. We've been able to help our customers improve forecasting accuracy. Can I share a brief story explaining how?

Not bad, huh? Takes less than 15 seconds, identifies who I am and whom I represent, refers to a problem common to the job title being called, infers credibility by referencing other customers, and asks permission to share a story about how I helped someone else. (Remember what can motivate mainstream buyers from Chapter 6, curiosity about peers and ego?)

So what if the prospect responds with a yes? You will need to be prepared and organized by having the related success story and having something like the conversational outline as shown in Table 11.1.

Table 11.1 Conversational Outline

Begin with:
Is now a good time to spend 10 or 15 minutes so I can learn more about you and your situation, or should we schedule something that works best for both of us?

If yes, share success story:	If no, offer other options:

[CustomerCentric Selling] helps companies [capture, codify, and implement their best selling and tactical marketing practices].
 	
   We were founded in [2002] and are a privately held [or publicly traded] company.
 	
   Some clients you may recognize include [client names].
 	
   Can you tell me more about you and your business?
	Other issues we hear from VPs of sales include:
	1. Lengthy time from new hire to first sale
	2. Wasting resources on unqualified opportunities
	3. 13 percent of the sales organization carrying the entire sales team

Continued on next page

Continued from previous page

	Are you interested in learning more about any of these issues?
	If yes:
	What I'd like to do is tell you about [that situation that you said you were interested in]. Then I'd like to learn more about you and your current situation.
	At that point we can make a mutual decision about whether or not further discussions are appropriate. Is that okay?
	If no:
	Thank you for your time. I look forward to checking back with you in a few months.

After sharing the success story, start by asking the question at the top of the table, "Is now a convenient time to spend 10 or 15 minutes . . . "

If after delivering the success story and your introduction, the prospect does not have the same or a similar problem, you will need to use the menu of goals on the right side of the conversational outline in an attempt to get the prospect to admit that there might be something—a goal, problem, or need—that he or she would like to discuss further. Remember our very first core concept: *no goal, no prospect.*

In Table 11.2, I list the primary problem that I lead with in my phone script and include the associated success story components directly below it. To the right of the primary problem is my menu of goals. All this is placed on one piece of paper. This is what I mean by being organized.

Table 11.2 Example Menu of Problems (from Target Conversation List)

Primary Problem	Menu Problem #1	Menu Problem #2	Menu Problem #3
Vice president of sales	Vice president of sales	Vice president of sales	Vice president of sales
Inability of salespeople to deliver on forecasted opportunities.	*Lengthy time from new hire to first sale.*	*Wasting resources on unqualified opportunities.*	*13 percent of salespeople carrying the entire group.*
Forecasting was totally subjective, relying strictly on the opinions of the salespeople.	"Sales training" was really only product training. Reps weren't taught *how* the product was used.	Resource requests were based on the opinion of the salesperson rather than tangible measures.	The most successful salespeople were promoted to management but were then unable to transfer skills.
The most successful salespeople were promoted to management but were then unable to transfer skills.	The ability to craft conversations in advance with appropriate biased diagnostic questions.	A series of questions for determining the viability of an opportunity before expending resources.	A defined road map that traditional salespeople can follow to mimic customer-centric behavior.
CustomerCentric Selling provided that capability.	CustomerCentric Selling provided that capability.	CustomerCentric Selling provided that capability.	CustomerCentric Selling provided that capability.
Forecast-to-close ratio went from 12 percent to 76 percent.	*Time from new hire to first sales decreased from 9 months to 3 months.*	*Demo-to-close ratio dropped from 4:1 to 9:1.*	*Percentage of salespeople achieving quota rose from 5 percent to 72 percent with no change in product or price.*

How to Use the Menu of Problems Tool

Let's say that I started by going through the first example in column 1 of Table 11.2. In this example, a sales manager was frustrated because her salespeople were not able to deliver on forecasted opportunities. I relayed this to the prospect and continued by describing the sales manager's former situation. "Forecasting was totally subjective, relying strictly on the opinions of the salespeople," I said. I continued quickly by adding, "The most successful salespeople were promoted to management but then were unable to transfer skills. CustomerCentric Selling provided that capability, and the forecast-to-close ratio went from 12 percent to 76 percent. But that was that manager's situation. Can you tell me about the challenges *you* are facing?"

As you can see, I have a structure to the call but can still deliver the call very conversationally. My aim is to have the prospects share their goal, problem, or need when I ask the question. If they do, we continue the conversation by asking insightful questions, listening, and continuing the sales process we teach in the CustomerCentric Selling methodology or whatever sales process you follow.

But what if they do not tell you about their situation? What if they say, "I don't have a problem like that"?

You quickly refer to your menu of problems listed in columns 2 to 4 in the table. For example, I might respond by saying, "That's good news. However, other concerns we hear from our clients include new sales reps taking too long to make their first sale, money and resources being wasted on unqualified opportunities, and a small number of sales reps producing virtually all the sales. Are you experiencing any of these issues?"

Again, when prospects say yes, I continue the sales conversation by asking and listening. Odds are that one of the problems will strike a nerve. Why? Because I have targeted a specific title in a specific industry within which we have expertise and knowledge of the issues. It makes sense that executives would be confronted by problems that plague their peers.

Still, sometimes nothing resonates with the prospect, and you have to move on. So what happens when all else fails and the prospect says no?

Keep things open for future communication by sending an e-mail similar to this:

Dear Stan:

I appreciate you taking the time to speak with me on the telephone earlier today. As I mentioned, the top three issues that our clients have asked CustomerCentric Selling to help them address include:

- Lengthy time from new hire to first sale
- Wasting resources on unqualified opportunities
- Ten percent of the sales team carrying the entire group

Clients whose names you might recognize, whom we have helped to successfully address these specific issues, include Knowlagent, Rockwell Automation, and Recondo Technology, to name just a few.

While I understand that these are not currently issues for you, should you begin to experience these or similar problems, I hope you will feel free to contact me. I've included my contact information at the end of this e-mail.

In the meantime, let's keep the line of communications open. I'll try to keep you up-to-date on what other [job titles] are telling us and where they are asking for our assistance. I've made a note to myself to call you in 60 days. I look forward to speaking with you again.

Regards,

Gary Walker

With this e-mail we have documented and confirmed what was discussed, dropped the names of some of our existing clients, invited the prospect to reengage should he or she experience the same or similar issues, told the prospect we are planning to continue to communicate with him or her by sharing what we are hearing from other senior executives, and noting that we plan to reengage with the prospect in 60 days. Executive contacts are difficult to make and should not be squandered. We want to develop and nurture the relationship.

Aligning with the Gatekeeper

At the start of this chapter, I revealed how much most salespeople detest prospecting. One of the things many salespeople dislike about the process is dealing with gatekeepers, whom they view as some sort of impenetrable force blocking access to the prospect.

It is not true. If you really think about it, gatekeepers could (and should) be your secret weapons in prospecting. In fact, I will make the argument that you may actually *want* to reach a gatekeeper. Here is why.

Like you, gatekeepers are professional people with a job to do. Just as you want to succeed and do well in your job, so do they. They do so by looking out for their boss, managing their boss's time, and providing pertinent information. This is where you come in.

If you can establish rapport with the gatekeeper, earn trust, demonstrate respect, and let him or her know about potential solutions to problems that the executive may be facing, the gatekeeper can personally benefit by being the one to present the potential solution to the executive. After all, the gatekeeper has personal and intimate knowledge of many of the company's problems, challenges, needs, and goals. Rather than being someone who blocks you, the gatekeeper could be, as I said, your secret weapon. Remember that the next time you encounter one, and *earn* the right to be his or her ally.

Start your call by asking for the person you want to speak to:

May I speak to Stan?

If the person says, "He is not available," you can ask for voice mail:

Could I leave him a voice mail?

For your voice-mail message, leave your telephone script.

If asked, "What is this regarding?" deliver a slightly modified script targeted to the gatekeeper:

I work with IT companies, and one of the primary concerns
I hear from senior sales executives is their frustration with

missed revenue targets due to inaccurate forecasts by sales-people. We have been able to help them deal with this issue, and I wanted to share with him how. Do you think this is something Stan might be interested in?

No matter if they respond yes or no, ask to send a letter of intro-duction:

I appreciate your taking the time to speak with me. I was wondering, if I sent a quick one-page letter (e-mail) introduc-ing myself and my company and recapping our conversation, would you be willing to take a look at it and tell me if it is anything you think Stan might be interested in?

E-mail or Letter to the Gatekeeper

You are probably thinking, "When did we transition from telephone prospecting to e-mail or letter?" We didn't. We are simply making it easier for the gatekeeper to deliver your message to the person he or she supports by preparing a written piece of correspondence. You don't want people to struggle to recollect what was discussed; you want to provide them with the exact message that you would like delivered. After the e-mail or letter has been sent, it provides you with another opportunity to follow up with the gatekeeper and determine the pros-pect executive's potential interest.

Some Additional Thoughts on Telephone Prospecting

Before moving on to the next method that I would like to discuss, here are some final points for you to consider:

- The telephone can be used as your only method of prospecting or as one of many methods that you will utilize in a multiple-method plan or campaign.

- Prospecting can and should be done within existing accounts. You should be able to leverage the existing relationship and current use of your product or services to your advantage. Don't squander it!
- Prospecting scripts lead with business issues or align with triggering events. They don't lead with what you are selling. It's all about the prospect.
- Call at decision-maker levels. The people at these levels are in the positions they are in to address problems and issues, and they can cause monies to be appropriated for unfunded initiatives.
- Manage the rejection and don't take it personally. It's not you they are rejecting; they are rejecting your intrusion on their time and space.
- The objective of your telephone prospecting is simply to gain "incremental interest." That interest may turn into a sales opportunity for you at some point.
- Be prepared in case the prospect says, "Tell me more!" There is nothing worse than the prospect being ready to go and you're not. Go back and revisit the discussion in the "Organizing to Prospect" section.
- Align and engage with the gatekeeper; it's the gatekeeper who has the keys to the kingdom.
- Document the conversation.
- Make it easy for the gatekeeper to relay the message.
- Create an opportunity for continued contact.
- If you are relegated to voice mail, embrace it! Use it to your advantage.
- Whenever you make contact, document and confirm your understanding of the call regardless of the level of interest. It's hard to make contacts, and this could be the start of a meaningful relationship.

Checkpoint #18

With telephone prospecting, should the focus be on quantity or quality?	

What are two things you should leave out of your telephone script?

1.

2.

What should you do if a buyer requests information instead of agreeing to a conversation?	
How can you remain in alignment with the person you are speaking with?	
What is the goal of asking questions from the menu of problems?	
What is the benefit of establishing rapport with the gatekeeper?	

Chapter 12

E-MAIL PROSPECTING

E-mail Prospecting 101

For many salespeople, e-mail has replaced the telephone as the prospecting tool of choice. Under increasing pressure to prospect and not wanting to do telephone prospecting, or having given up on it, salespeople have turned to e-mail as a way to demonstrate that they are doing something—and who knows, you might get someone to engage. However, we've talked a number of times in this book about what we are looking for in our own e-mail mailbox and how we deal with the unsolicited e-mails that we receive. Despite that fact, salespeople continue to use this method without regard for the consequences. This being the reality, let's explore the pros and cons:

Pros

- *E-mail is fast.* First, your production time is minimal . . . about the time it takes you to write it. Second, you hit "Send" and your message is delivered almost instantly. And third, if your message is compelling or provocative, you may begin receiving instantaneous feedback and responses.

- *E-mail is inexpensive.* This is one of the reasons salespeople and marketing like it. Even if the response rate is marginal, the cost is minimal.
- *Your attachments are instantly available.* If you want to deliver a success story, white paper, etc., it only takes a couple of mouse clicks and you have delivered your content.
- *You can test its effectiveness.* I think this is a key benefit. Due to the speed and the cost, it is a great way to test your Sales Ready Messaging on different groups, different job titles, different issues, different triggering events, etc. It's a way to determine what seems to be resonating with your targeted individuals.

Cons

- *People are inundated with e-mail = delete!* People skim their inbox looking for e-mail from colleagues, family, friends, or someone they are waiting to hear from. If you don't fall into one of those four categories, you are *deleted.*
- *Spam filters provide a first line of defense.* Because people are inundated with e-mail, e-mail systems are equipped with elaborate spam filters that prevent your e-mail from ever reaching their inbox. Sometimes spam filters even filter out legitimate e-mails. I know that I check my junk folder daily for relevant e-mails that I may have missed.
- *Salespeople hide behind their e-mails.* I mentioned this earlier, that I think salespeople use e-mailing as their sole method of prospecting because it is fast and easy and allows them to remain somewhat immune from the personal rejection they experience when they use the telephone. It also allows them to demonstrate to their management that they are doing some prospecting. In reality, they are hiding behind their e-mails. They are taking an easier, but ineffective, way out.
- *E-mails need to be short.* When prospects are going through their e-mails, they want information quickly. Long copy is out. Complex offers are out. Supporting facts and arguments are out.

- *They limit your creativity.* An all-text e-mail is boring. So your message is it. Your message has *to be aligned with your* recipient's goals, problems, and issues. Remember, it is about them, not you!

E-mail Prospecting: Format and Content of the E-mails

It's essential to tend to both format and content when creating e-mails.

Format

The format should be clear and "clean looking"—easy to read!

Keep It Simple

- Use plain text only (no graphics, etc.). You are *communicating*, not marketing. Your message is what is going to create interest, not the graphics or attachments.
- Use large enough type so that it shows up clearly in the preview window.

Content

The length of the e-mail and the opportunity for discussion are elements you need to address, but you'll first want to focus on the subject line since that will determine if people will even open the e-mail.

Subject Line

- Brand your e-mails, e.g., CustomerCentric Selling and First Software.
- Avoid gimmicks (URGENT, etc.).
- If this is a referral, note it here first.
- The goal is to get recipients to open your message.

Shorter Is Better

- People may be viewing their e-mails on their smartphone.
- Reference other clients—leverage the "herd mentality."
- Offer specific, measurable results.

Include a Relevant Call to Action

- Offer an opportunity to have a discussion.
- If not the correct person to engage with, ask for a referral to someone else.
- Offer to contact the person's administrative assistant (by name, if possible) to schedule further contact.
- Invite them to "simply hit reply" to respond to your message or schedule a convenient time to speak on the telephone.

E-mail Prospecting: Three-E-mail Series

Sending out a single good e-mail and expecting that someone will engage with you is an unrealistic expectation. I'm not saying it won't happen, but the chances are very slim. It takes more than a single e-mail message to obtain some mindshare. There are all sorts of opinions on just how many times you will have to "touch" someone before he or she will engage.

One of my preferred approaches is to prepare three e-mails for each prospect. Each successive e-mail builds upon or references the preceding e-mail. Of course, this is only relevant if the prospects don't respond to the earlier e-mails. If they do, great! I start the process from that point. Otherwise, here is a three-e-mail-series approach that has proved quite successful:

E-mail #1

- Send to *all* executives simultaneously.
- Reference other clients—clients within the same market, whose names might be recognizable. Name-dropping doesn't hurt.
- Ask for response or redirection. If the recipient isn't the responsible person, invite him or her to redirect you to the correct person to deal with your inquiry. The redirection becomes a referral. We'll speak more to this later.
- Commit to telephone follow-up. Let the recipients know that you intend to call them and when.

Or

- Invite them to select "Reply." An additional option is to ask them to simply select "Reply" to redirect you, communicate with you directly, etc.

E-mail #2

- *Send this one day prior to the telephone follow-up.* It reminds the prospect that the call is pending.
- *Include a menu of problems.* Share with the prospect other issues that you are being asked by your clients to help them address.

E-mail #3

- *This is the final e-mail.* Let the prospects know that this will be your last attempt to contact them. They shouldn't have to think that every time they check their e-mail there will be yet another e-mail from you. Additionally, it's letting them know that this is their last opportunity to easily connect with you about an issue of importance.
- *Include references.* Provide not just client names, but also quotes from success stories that you can repurpose and use in your e-mail campaign.

Example: Prospecting E-mail Series

Up to this point, the examples that I have shared with you have been based on CustomerCentric Selling and on the goals, problems, and needs of senior sales executives. I'm going to use this opportunity to share with you a three e-mail series I developed while working with a salesperson for TrialStat, who attended one of our public workshops.

TrialStat is a leading provider of on-demand, electronic-data-capture applications that empower clinical research companies and professionals to collect and manage clinical data faster using the TrialStat application. To learn more about TrialStat, visit the company's website at http://www.trialstat.com.

The salesperson that I was working with didn't want to have to rely on marketing for all his leads and wanted to proactively expand the number of opportunities entering his sales pipeline.

E-mail #1

Subject: "Why does our trial completion date continue to slip?"

Dear [name]:

Sound familiar? Are you under increasing pressure to complete your clinical trials on time and within budget? Are regulatory oversights placing your company at financial risk? Are these oversights creating more FDA attention than you feel is needed? Are your clinical trials taking longer to complete than you promised?

TrialStat is in the business of helping pharmaceutical companies accelerate clinical trials, improve regulatory compliance, and reduce overall trial expense through the products and services we provide. Some of our clients whose names you might recognize include ABC Pharmaceuticals, DEF Pharma, and GHI, Inc.

Some of the chief concerns we have been hearing from the clinical trial and operations executives we have worked with include:

- "The amount of time it takes for us to meet, train, and test investigators and physicians adds months to our clinical trials. Investigator turnover exacerbates this problem."
- "Trial protocols change frequently based on trial findings. It's taking my staff weeks to create, distribute, verify receipt, and confirm understanding of new trial documentation sent to all IRBs, investigators, and regulatory groups."
- "Collecting regulatory documents is a nightmare! We have to deal with multiple time zones, lost overnight packages, manual tracing, and countless phone calls. There has to be a better way!"

We have been able to help our clients successfully deal with these issues. If you have some of these same concerns and would like to share with me your situation, simply select "Reply" to schedule a mutually convenient time for us to speak on the telephone, or give me a call at (866) 416-STAT.

Sincerely,

Salesperson, TrialStat, Inc.

E-mail #2

Subject: "You need to get a handle on your trial costs!"

Dear Joe Prospect:

In my previous e-mail to you dated [date], I shared with you that TrialStat, Inc., has helped other senior clinical trial and operations executives in the pharmaceutical industry solve some very difficult challenges.

TrialStat has helped pharmaceutical companies shorten the time required to complete their clinical trials, improve their ability to comply with FDA regulations, and reduce overall trial expense through our products and services.

I would like to ask if your clinical trial meets any of the following characteristics:

- Does your clinical trial process require the continual exchange of information among scientists, physicians, patients, investigators, and regulatory agencies?
- Do you spend more time and expense traveling to and from investigator meetings than you do in the actual meetings themselves?
- Does it take your staff weeks to create, distribute, verify receipt, and confirm understanding of new trial documentation sent to all IRBs, investigators, and regulatory groups?
- During Phase II or Phase III, are you required to send out hundreds of regulatory packages to investigators, resulting in increased trial expense?

- Are you under increasing pressure during Phase IV of your clinical trial to quickly identify and validate competitive differentiators that could maximize your drug's revenue contribution?

If you answered yes to any of the above questions, then TrialStat may be able to help you and your organization. If you would like to learn how, please give me a call at (866) 416-STAT, and I will provide you with a free case study prepared by *eyeonpharma* detailing how we have helped another pharmaceutical manufacturer deal with these very issues.

Sincerely,

Salesperson, TrialStat, Inc.

E-mail #3

Subject: My e-mails to you dated [put dates in if you have them]

Dear Joe Prospect:

In my previous two e-mails to you, I indicated that TrialStat, Inc., has helped clinical trial and operations executives in the pharmaceutical industry accelerate clinical trials, improve regulatory compliance, and reduce overall trial expense through the products and services we provide. In this, my final e-mail to you, I would like to share some of the comments our clients (and your peers) have made about TrialStat online collaboration capabilities.

"In clinical trials that take years and cost millions of dollars, every day saved can result in therapeutic alternatives for patients and significant cost savings for the company. TrialStat emerged as one solution that could produce concrete time and cost savings, and we are now implementing its use in clinical trials. Through the use of TrialStat's services, we will greatly enhance information exchange among IRBs,

CROs, investigators, and trial managers, and hope to accelerate the process significantly. We anticipate that the results of this initiative will be enormously successful."

Vice President, US Clinical Development

(ABC) Pharmaceuticals

"TrialStat's new capabilities have enabled us to transform our processes for investigator meetings by completing the training and testing of physicians online. We have been able to reach out to a greater number of potential investigator sites, while reducing the number of investigator meetings and increasing flexibility and convenience for physicians. Over 400 of our study recruits have elected to participate in the training and testing option offered online through TrialStat."

RN Medical Product Manager with US Medical Research

(DEF) Pharmaceuticals

"By moving the due diligence process online with TrialStat, we were able to greatly enhance collaboration among the various groups and complete the due diligence faster. TrialStat allowed us to distribute sensitive information and answer questions in a more timely fashion, while eliminating the costs and security concerns associated with paper, faxes, and e-mails."

Group Business and Planning

(GHI) Pharmaceuticals

Joe, I'm confident that we could assist you in obtaining these same types of improvements. I'll be calling your administrative assistant to schedule a mutually agreeable time to speak with you about your current trial situation and the associated challenges you have been directed to address. In the meantime, if you have any questions, please call me. My telephone number and other contact information are located below.

Sincerely,

A. Salesperson, TrialStat, Inc.

In this series of e-mails, a conscious decision was made to be a little provocative. The subjects of the first two e-mails were made to appear as questions that could be posed to someone who is responsible for conducting a clinical trial that might not be going well. The content of each e-mail talks about common problems and issues that contribute to clinical trials taking too long or becoming too expensive. The two e-mails end with an invitation to engage with the TrialStat salesperson if the prospect is experiencing any of the same problems or issues. Both are an attempt to align with the prospect. There is nothing about what the salesperson is selling. It's a customer-centric approach.

If selling is a "hurt and rescue" mission, then the first two e-mails are *hurt* and the third e-mail is the *rescue*. The rescue is in the form of what other senior executives, same industry, similar job titles, have been able to accomplish using TrialStat's capabilities.

It's an excellent creative example of an e-mail series developed around all the ideas, principles, and concepts we have discussed so far. I'd also encourage you to be creative in your approach.

Targeted E-mail Example: Triggering Event— Change in Sales Leadership

The preceding e-mail series was based on the salesperson's knowledge of his marketplace and the typical problems and issues associated with that market. This next e-mail is very different; this is an attempt to take advantage of *what you know* by taking advantage of a triggering event and engaging with prospects at their time of need.

In this example, we are going to take advantage of a triggering event by utilizing monitoring technologies like Google Alert, iLantern, InsideView, and Lead411. Any one of these technologies might have alerted the salesperson to the triggering event—a *change in sales leadership*.

As previously discussed in Chapter 7 under "There Is a New Sheriff in Town," this change probably took place because the preceding sales leader was relieved from his position and then replaced. That is not always the case, but frequently it is. One of the nice things about press releases is that, in addition to naming the new executive, the announcement is typically made by the hiring executive; this is the person who probably had to move against the former vice president of sales and who has given specific instructions to the newly appointed vice president about what needs to be accomplished. This gives the salesperson two people to try to engage with!

E-mail to the New Hire
Here is the first e-mail to the newly appointed vice president of sales.

Subject: "First Software Appoints Jim Smith to VP Sales"

Dear Jim:

I saw the announcement of your appointment on *MarketWire* and wanted to congratulate you on becoming the new Vice President of Sales for First Software!

I'm going to assume that you have inherited *a sales organization that needs your help*. Is that correct?

I have seen a number of changes in sales leadership over the last few months, and I have had the opportunity to speak with quite a few of these new senior sales executives. The top five complaints that I have been hearing from them (I have to paraphrase here) include:

1. "The company has no defined sales process. The salespeople want to do their own thing."
2. "My salespeople are spending too much time attempting to sell to people who can't buy our offering."
3. "Too many good sales opportunities are being lost to 'no decision.'"
4. "Selling to my reps means discounting until the prospect says yes."

5. "I'm tired of my salespeople blaming their losses on the economy."

Are you inheriting any of these same difficulties? Recognizing that you need time to settle in and assess your situation, I will call you Thursday, June 1, to see if I can be of any assistance to you. However, if you have already concluded you have some issues you need to address, *then just select "Reply" and send me a quick note,* and I will call you to schedule a mutually agreeable time to talk with you on the phone.

I look forward to hearing from you.

Regards,

Gary Walker
CustomerCentric Selling

E-mail to the Hiring Manager

Here is the e-mail to the hiring manager or other person who made the announcement.

Dear Sam:

I saw the press release on *MarketWire* and wanted to congratulate you on the selection of Jim Smith as your new Vice President of Sales. Based on my brief review of his experience and background, he appears to be well suited to the task of improving the sales and revenue performance of the First Software sales organization.

Over the last three months I've had the opportunity to speak with a number of newly appointed senior sales executives. Even though they have been in their positions for only a short period of time, the top five concerns that I've been hearing from them (I have to paraphrase here) include:

- "The company has no defined sales process. The salespeople want to do their own thing."

- "My salespeople gravitate toward end users. They are spending too much time attempting to sell to people who can't buy our offering."
- "Too many good sales opportunities are being lost to 'no decision.'"
- "Selling to these reps means discounting until the prospect says yes."
- "I'm tired of my salespeople blaming their losses on the economy."

Is First Software experiencing any of the same difficulties I described above? Are these some of the same issues you have directed Jim to correct?

I've sent a similar e-mail to Jim, and recognizing that he needs time to settle in and assess his situation, I'll call him in a few days to see if I can be of any assistance to him. If you have any insights that you would like to share with me, I would like to hear from you also. Simply hit "Reply" and we can schedule a time to speak on the telephone.

Regards,

Gary Walker
CustomerCentric Selling

Attachments: Knovel success story and CustomerCentric Selling overview

Second E-mail to the New Hire

Here is a second e-mail that I'm prepared to send to Jim in the event that he won't engage with me when I call.

Subject: First Software's Sales Performance

Dear Jim:

I'm following up on the e-mail I sent you back on May 23, after the announcement of your appointment as the Vice President of Sales for First Software.

I have found that when you take on a position like you have, for about the first 60 days, you are able to attribute the sales organization's ongoing performance problems to your predecessor. On or about day 61, if performance hasn't changed, then you become accountable for any sales performance problems that continue to exist.

If you are continuing to struggle with some of the performance issues you inherited, you can either attempt to go it alone or look for some assistance. Do any of your goals for First Software include:

- Having your salespeople engage with senior-level buyers versus low-level users
- Increasing the number of salespeople who operate above quota
- Achieving accurate revenue forecasting at the opportunity level
- Shortening sales cycles
- Eliminating or reducing discounting
- Reducing the cost of sales

If so, I'm confident that I can help. However, we won't know until I know what you are dealing with and what you would like to accomplish with the sales team. That's going to require a *conversation*. I'll call you on June 6 to schedule a mutually agreeable time for us to speak on the telephone. If you would like to schedule that telephone call now, just select "Reply" and send me a quick e-mail, and I will call you to schedule a mutually agreeable time to talk with you on the phone.

I have attached a couple of success stories so that you can see what we have helped some of our other clients accomplish.

Regards,

Gary Walker
CustomerCentric Selling

Attachments: Knovel, Inc., and L-3 Commercial InfraRed success stories

Again this is another variation of the previous e-mails. However, it too builds upon the ideas, principles, and concepts expressed so far in this book. The e-mails are both a little provocative, such as "you have inherited a sales organization that needs your help" and "On or about day 61, if performance hasn't changed, then you become accountable for any sales performance problems that continue to exist." That is, in fact, the reality of the situation. The prospect knows it, and the seller knows it. Some salespeople dance around the issues; I'm suggesting that you confront them directly. You want to be viewed as different from your competitors and competent and knowledgeable in your approach.

In both e-mails the prospect was invited to engage immediately by selecting "Reply" and was notified that the salesperson would be calling. So this campaign consisted of potentially three e-mails and two phone calls.

While we know that an e-mail followed by a phone call is only marginally more effective than just a telephone call, this example adds a couple of additional variables that improve its effectiveness:

- Initiating contact based on a triggering event
- Attempting to engage with the targeted executive's superior
- Using messaging that is somewhat provocative and direct

One last thing—if you say in your e-mail that you are going to call the prospect on a particular date, *make sure you follow through*. Put the follow-up call on your to-do list or Outlook calendar.

Checkpoint #19

What format should your e-mails be in?	
How many e-mails should be included in your e-mail prospecting series?	

Continued on next page

Continued from previous page

Your e-mails should be used to initiate contact based on what?	
Your messaging should be _____ and _____.	

Chapter *13*

FIVE-STEP PROSPECTING METHODOLOGY

Adding the Five-Step Prospecting Methodology into the Mix

In the previous two chapters, we discussed both telephone and e-mail prospecting. In an attempt to increase the effectiveness of both those methods, I introduced the idea of initiating contact based on a triggering event—contacting the superior of the person you want to engage with, using messaging that is provocative and is aligned with what motivates mainstream buyers, and using an e-mail or letter to document and confirm the conversation, as well as enlist the aid of a gatekeeper you may have spoken with.

Now what I'd like to do is to combine those two minimally effective methods to increase their effectiveness. We are going to do this by adding a new process, a series of steps complete with timing that you can execute. In addition to increasing the effectiveness of the two methods, there is the added benefit of increasing your productivity, since you will know what you are going to do and when you are going to do it.

This is a simple, easy-to-execute, five-step prospecting campaign that:

- Is developed around a triggering event to engage with an individual(s)
- Utilizes multiple methods, such as e-mail and telephone
- Requires both e-mail and telephone or voice-mail scripting to be developed in advance
- Introduces the concept of multiple touches over a condensed period of time to obtain mindshare and create a sense of urgency

Here is what I mean. In the example we will explore below, we are going to make five attempts to contact a Key Player over a 10-day period, once every 48 hours.

1. We are going to *send an initial e-mail to a Key Player* referencing the *triggering event* with an *electronic call to action*:
   - Engage directly now by selecting "Reply" or calling.
   - Request to be referred—to forward the e-mail—to the correct person with responsibility for dealing with the triggering event.
2. Make a *warm telephone call* to the Key Player you are attempting to reach.
   - It should be scripted.
3. *With your next e-mail, include an attachment with a success story* that aligns with and relates to the triggering event.
4. Make a prospecting *telephone call utilizing your menu of goals.*
5. Send an *e-mail to the Key Player and other job titles who constitute your sphere of influence.*

There is some debate among prospectors about whether or not you should advise your prospects with each subsequent contact that you have attempted to contact them previously. My position is yes— that with each subsequent contact you should advise your prospects that you have attempted to contact them previously. I'm attempting to establish my competency and my company's competency, as well as obtain mindshare. I recommend that you remind the prospects of your previous attempts to contact them in all, or at least some, of your subsequent contacts. You'll see what I mean in the following example campaign.

Five-Step Prospecting Campaign

Let's look at the five-step process that we suggest you use. We are going to employ a number of variables—multiple methods, frequency, message, and the use of a triggering event—in an effort to get our prospect to engage.

Step 1. Short E-mail Based on a Triggering Event

In this step, there are three major points to focus on:

- Beginning the subject line with "Your . . ."
- Adhering to the three-scroll rule
- Ending with a simple question

The subject line of an e-mail goes a long way in determining if it will be opened and read. Subject lines that begin with "Your . . ." and that reference the triggering event help to relate immediately to the prospect. The body of the e-mail should be readable with a maximum of three clicks on a PDA, should include a signature line with just your name and company, and should have a call to action that is easy for the buyer to take (e.g., hitting "Reply" to schedule a mutually agreeable time to speak on the telephone or asking to be referred to the appropriate person). You may also want to e-mail a higher-level person than your target title. Avoid using graphics and attachments. If successful, the targeted person will engage, or you may be referred to someone else.

Example: Triggering Event = Newly Hired or Newly Promoted Key Player

Subject: Your Promotion to VP of Sales for First Software

Dear Jim:

I'm assuming that you have inherited an underperforming sales team and will be held accountable for getting it fixed. Implementing a defined sales process that salespeople can be taught to execute, and that managers can be taught to inspect and coach, can result in organizational revenue goals being met and exceeded.

Simply hit "Reply" if you'd like to schedule time to speak on the telephone, or direct me to the person who is responsible for sales performance improvement.

Regards,

Gary Walker
CustomerCentric Selling

Step 2. Warm Telephone Call—Scripted

This step is used whether you connect directly with the person, reach voice mail, or have a conversation with a personal assistant or other gatekeeper. It should establish that you have attempted to contact the prospect previously. Your message should align with the triggering event.

We refer to this second contact as potentially being warm because the prospect may have seen or have recalled receiving and reading all or part of your initial e-mail.

Example: Triggering Event = Newly Hired or Newly Promoted Key Player

This is . . .	Gary Walker
with . . .	CustomerCentric Selling. You may recall receiving an e-mail from me on [day and date].

One of the chief concerns I'm hearing from other . . .	Newly appointed VPs of sales
Is their frustration with . . .	A lack of organizational sales process resulting in revenue goals not being met.
We've [I've] been able to help our customers . . .	Deal with their issues, and I would like an opportunity to share with you how.

Step 3. Success Story That Aligns with and Relates to a Triggering Event

By this time the Key Player you have been trying to reach has heard from you on two previous occasions. We believe that in this third attempt to reach the person, he or she may benefit from learning how you have helped someone else, same job title, similar industry, similar situation, effectively deal with the problem. This e-mail will include a success story as an attachment.

Example: Triggering Event = Newly Hired or Newly Promoted Key Player

Subject: Your Promotion to VP of Sales for First Software

Dear Jim:

I've attempted to contact you on two previous occasions but have been unsuccessful.

Taking an underperforming sales team and correcting the performance of the team members is now your sole responsibility. I have attached a brief success story that documents what Knowlagent's new Vice President of Sales, Kevin Kiernan, was able to accomplish with our help. It shouldn't take you more than two minutes to read.

If you would like to share with me what you have inherited, simply hit "Reply" at the top of your screen if you'd like to schedule time to speak on the telephone. If the responsibility for sales performance improvement falls elsewhere within the organization, please direct me to the right person.

Regards,

Gary Walker
CustomerCentric Selling

Attachment: Knowlagent success story

Step 4. Prospecting Call with a Menu of Goals

In this fourth attempt, you are going to try to reach the prospect by telephone again. Because the call is scripted, you can deliver the script to the Key Player or to the administrative assistant (requires some delivery modifications), or you can leave it on the person's voice mail. We are going to build the script around the top three issues and a menu of goals that you believe this person or job title could be experiencing in his or her new role.

Example: Triggering Event = Newly Hired or Newly Promoted Key Player

This is. . . .	Gary Walker
With . . .	CustomerCentric Selling. I've attempted to contact you on three previous occasions over the last several days but have been unsuccessful.
The top three complaints that I have been hearing from . . .	Newly appointed VPs of sales
Include:	"Too many good opportunities are being lost to 'no decision.'" "Selling to these reps means discounting until the prospects says yes." "Lack of a defined sales process makes it virtually impossible to provide opportunity coaching."

We've [I've] been able to help our customers . . .	Deal with their issues, and I would like an opportunity to share with you how.
(Example: Voice-mail option)	If you would like to share with me what you have inherited, you can call me at (800) 993-1228 or simply hit "Reply" to send me an e-mail to schedule a more convenient date and time for us to speak.

Step 5. Sphere-of-Influence E-mail

In this, your final attempt, you are contacting your Key Player as well as those individuals who you believe can buy, fund, and implement or activate your offering, and you are encouraging them to engage. You are not referencing the triggering event or previous attempts; you are simply trying to see if any of the people who could be affected by an underperforming sales organization will engage. As a result, the subject line will be different, but it will align with the previous voice-mail and e-mail message.

Example: Triggering Event = Newly Hired or Newly Promoted Key Player

Subject: First Software's Sales Performance

Dear Jim:

I'm sending this final e-mail to you, Reed Henry, and Barry White to find out who is responsible for sales performance improvement initiatives at First Software.

CustomerCentric Selling is in the business of helping underperforming sales organizations achieve revenue goals, shorten sales cycles, minimize discounting, and improve forecasting accuracy through the implementation and use of our sales process.

Representative clients include Aspen Technology, Knovel, L-3 Security and Detections Systems, MapQuest, and Rockwell Automation. These companies have successfully used

CustomerCentric Selling to increase productivity and sales effectiveness while reducing overall cost by integrating marketing and sales efforts more effectively.

I would like to schedule a 30-minute conference call to introduce you to our organization and to share with you how our clients in your industry have benefited from CustomerCentric Selling. To schedule a mutually agreeable time to speak on the telephone, simply select "Reply" to respond to this e-mail. If this responsibility falls elsewhere within the organization, please direct me to the appropriate person.

Regards,

Gary Walker
CustomerCentric Selling

Attachment: [Client] success story

Here are some additional thoughts you'll want to bear in mind when using this approach:

- Build the campaign based on the triggering event that you have identified as being a reason to engage.
- Your campaign should be scripted (e-mails and voice mails) in advance.
- The scripts should be aligned with what is important to your prospect.
- Be provocative, not offensive, with your message.
- Your efforts must be timed and executed correctly—5 touches over 10 days.
- It will require multiple touches before you begin to gain mindshare.
- Use available technology within your SFA or CRM to store and deliver your e-mail series.
- Monitor your performance. Some applications tell you if your e-mails are being opened, read, or forwarded.
- Don't be afraid to modify your message and timing to obtain a better result. As a matter of fact, it's a necessity.

- Determine what resonates with your prospects.
- Don't rely on this five-step approach exclusively. Think of it as just another tool that is available to you.

Checkpoint #20

What are the five steps of prospecting? 1. 2. 3. 4. 5.	
You should build your prospecting campaign around what?	
What is required to create a sense of urgency and obtain mindshare?	

Chapter *14*

THUNDER AND LIGHTNING

Up to this point we have talked about telephone and e-mail as prospecting methods; we have explored their advantages and disadvantages, explained how you can attempt to enhance their effectiveness by using them to engage your prospects at their time of need, described the directness and tone of the messages that you use, and discussed the timing and frequency with which you use them. Now I'd like to introduce you to yet another variable that I have found to be very effective as part of my own daily prospecting activities. I call it *thunder and lightning*—the synchronous use of the telephone and e-mail.

Tell me if this, or something like this, has ever happened to you. You are sitting at your desk working on a project, an assignment, when you realize that you don't have all the information you need to continue. You think, where and how can I get that information? Then it dawns on you that one of your coworkers has the information you need. You quickly pick up your telephone and dial his number. It rings, rings, rings, and you finally receive a voice-mail greeting advising you that your coworker is not available and inviting you to leave a message following the beep. Disappointed, you leave your message: "John, it's Gary. I'm working on a project, working against a deadline. You have information that I need in order to complete it. Please call me as soon as you get this message." Concerned that John may not check his voice messages or is out of the office, you draft a quick e-mail: "John, I don't know if you are in your office, but I just called and left you a voice message. I'm working on a project, working against a deadline, and you have a critical piece of information that I need in order to complete it. Please call me as soon as you get this message." Then you press "Send." You sit back in your chair thinking about how to proceed without the needed information when all of a sudden your phone rings. It's John: "Sorry I wasn't available when you called; I was tied up. However, I just saw your e-mail and wanted to get back to you. What information are you looking for?"

I'm going to assume that the scenario I described . . . working on a project, missing information . . . is not identical to what you experienced. But how about your needing to speak with someone, placing the telephone call, leaving the voice message, and then, concerned that your message may not be retrieved, sending off a quick e-mail—and within seconds you receive a phone call or e-mail from the person you were trying to reach. Has that ever happened to you?

Do you think all those unanswered phone calls you make and recorded messages you hear when you call are because the people you are trying to reach are not in their offices? Think again. When you get down to the bare facts, the people you were trying to reach were in their office; they just weren't answering their telephone. Either they recognized who it was or they didn't; they simply chose not to answer their phone. However, when they saw the corresponding message pop up on their e-mail, they were moved to action.

I call this method of using the telephone and e-mail synchronously *thunder and lightning!* You have heard the expression, "The whole is greater than the sum of its parts." This is a perfect example. You will find that when you leave a carefully crafted, short telephone script, followed instantly and synchronously with an aligned and carefully crafted e-mail, your ability to get your prospect to engage with you goes up exponentially.

Voice Mail and E-mail = Thunder and Lightning!

Together, the following voice-mail scripts and e-mail models serve as an example of a *thunder-and-lightning* series built around first a single high-probability issue, followed by a menu of goals. The series could just as easily have been built around a triggering event.

Voice-Mail Script #1: Leave a Message Referencing Other Clients

This is Gary Walker with CustomerCentric Selling. I recently helped L-3 Communications Infrared Products implement a defined sales process to achieve greater accuracy in its revenue forecast. I thought you might be interested in learning more about how we've helped L-3 Communications improve forecasting accuracy into the 95th percentile.

If you are interested in learning how we've helped organizations such as L-3 Communications achieve these results, please call me at (800) 993-1228, extension 702. Again, my name is Gary Walker, and my number is (800) 993-1228, extension 702.

Instant E-mail #1: Thunder and Lightning!

_____, I just this moment attempted to reach you by telephone, but I was unsuccessful. If you look at your caller ID, you will see a missed call and a voice mail from me.

I recently helped L-3 Communications Infrared Products implement a defined sales process that allowed the company to increase its revenue forecasting accuracy to 95 percent.

I'm at my desk right now if you would like to call me. My number is (800) 993-1228, extension 702. If this is not a good time, simply select "Reply" and propose an alternative date and time. I look forward to speaking with you. In the meantime, I have attached a success story that recounts what L-3 Communications Infrared Products has been able to accomplish.

Regards,

Gary Walker
CustomerCentric Selling

Attachment: L-3 Communications success story

Voice-Mail Script #2: Leave a Message Listing a Menu of Problems

This is Gary Walker. I recently left you a message regarding how we helped L-3 Communications Infrared Products improve its sales forecasting accuracy. The top three issues that we are being asked by other senior sales executives to help them address are:

1. Lengthy time from new hire to first sale
2. Wasting resources on unqualified opportunities
3. Ten percent of the sales team carrying the entire sales organization

If you are interested in learning how we've helped these organizations achieve these results, please call me at (800) 993-1228, extension 702. Again, my name is Gary Walker, and my number is (800) 993-1228, extension 702.

Instant E-mail #2: Thunder and Lightning!

_____, I just this moment attempted to reach you by telephone but I was unsuccessful. If you look at your caller ID, you will see a missed call from me and a voice mail. The top three issues we are being asked by other senior sales executives to help them address are:

1. Lengthy time from new hire to first sale
2. Wasting resources on unqualified opportunities
3. Ten percent of the sales team carrying the entire sales organization

I'm at my desk right now if you would like to call me. My number is (800) 993-1228, extension 702. If this is not a good time, simply select "Reply" and propose an alternative date and time. I look forward to speaking with you. In the meantime, I have attached another success story that recounts what we've been able to help our clients accomplish.

Regards,

Gary Walker
CustomerCentric Selling

Attachment: [Client] success story

Voice-Mail Script #3: "This Is My Last Call to You"

This is Gary Walker. Over the last four days, I have left you two messages regarding how we have helped sales leadership deal with some difficult sales performance issues. Despite my requests, to date I have not heard back from you. I want you to know that this will be the last voice message I will leave you.

If you are interested in learning how world-class companies are differentiating themselves based on how they sell, rather than attempting to get by on product features and functions, please call me at (800) 993-1228, extension 702. Again, my name is Gary Walker, and my number is (800) 993-1228, extension 702.

Instant E-mail #3: Thunder and Lightning!

_____, I just this moment attempted to reach you by telephone for the third time, but I was unsuccessful. CustomerCentric Selling is in the business of helping our customers improve business results by helping them define and implement a consistent, repeatable "sales process" (1) that salespeople can be taught to execute, (2) that you can monitor, coach, and inspect, and (3) that represents your most effective and best sales practices. The last thing that I want to do is be viewed as an annoyance by leaving you voice messages or e-mailing you repeatedly.

In this, my final correspondence to you, I would like to ask if you would like to speak with me now. I'm at my desk right now. If you would like to call me, my number is (800) 993-1228, extension 702. If this is not a good time, simply select "Reply" and propose an alternative date and time.

Regards,

Gary Walker
CustomerCentric Selling

Attachment: CustomerCentric Selling overview

Exercise 9. Thunder and Lightning!

In an effort to help you collect your thoughts and develop your own thunder-and-lightning series, I've created an exercise that mirrors the example that I just shared with you. That example began with my attempting to engage the prospect by using a *high-probability issue*, something that I know the person is more than likely experiencing, and then I proceeded to use a menu of goals (three additional high-probability issues). But the entire campaign could also have been developed around—and the messaging developed to exploit—a specific *triggering event* that you have determined is your prospect's time of need. I use triggering events very successfully when I've made aware of a change in sales leadership.

Leave a Message (Voice-Mail Script #1) Referencing Other Clients

This is . . .	[Your name]
With . . .	[Your company's name]
I recently helped . . .	[Client name/do what?]
I thought you might be interested in learning how we helped . . .	[Client name/accomplish what/measureable result]
If you are interested in learning how we helped this organization achieve these results, please call me at . . .	[Your number]
Again, my name is . . .,	[Your name]
And my number is . . .	[Your number]

Instant E-mail #1: Thunder and Lightning!

_____, I just this moment attempted to reach you by telephone but was unsuccessful. If you look at your caller ID, you will see a missed call from me and a voice message waiting. I recently helped [client name/do what].

I'm at my desk right now if you would like to call me. My number is [your phone number]. If this is not a good time, simply select "Reply" at the top of your screen and propose an alternative date and time. I look forward to speaking with you. In the meantime, I have attached a success story that recounts what [client name] has been able to accomplish.

Regards,

[Your name]

Attachment: Success story

Exercise 9a. Leave a Message (Voice-Mail Script #2) Listing a Menu of Problems

This is . . .	[Your name]
I recently left you a message* regarding how we helped . . .	[Client name/accomplish what/ measureable result]
The top three issues that we are being asked by other senior . . .	[Job title]
To help them address are . . . 1. 2. 3.	

Continued on next page

Continued from previous page

If you are interested in learning how we helped these executives successfully address these issues, please call me at . . .	[Your number]
Again, my name is . . .	[Your name]
and my number is . . .	[Your number]

*If you would like, you can tell the prospect the exact day and date you left the message.

Instant E-mail #2: Thunder and Lightning!

_____, I just this moment attempted to reach you by telephone but was unsuccessful. If you look at your caller ID, you will see a missed call from me and a voice message waiting. The top three issues we are being asked by other senior executives to help them address are:

1.
2.
3.

I'm at my desk right now if you would like to call me. My number is [your phone number]. If this is not a good time, simply select "Reply" at the top of your screen and propose an alternative date and time. I look forward to speaking with you. In the meantime, I have attached another success story that recounts what [client name] has been able to accomplish.

Regards,

[Your name]

Attachment: Success story

Exercise 9b. "This Is My Last Call to You" (Voice-Mail Script #3)

This is . . .	[Your name]
Over the last . . .	[Number of days]
Days I have left you two messages regarding how we have helped . . .	[Senior executive job title]
Despite my repeated attempts to contact you, to date I have not heard back from you. I want you to know that this will be the last voice message that I will leave you.	
If you are interested in learning how we have helped . . .	[Companies do what]
Please call me at . . .	[Your number]
Again, my name is . . .	[Your name]
and my number is . . .	[Your number]

Instant E-mail #3: Thunder and Lightning!

_____, I just this moment attempted to reach you by telephone for the third time, but I was unsuccessful.

[Company name] is in the business of helping our customers . . .

The last thing I want to do is be viewed as an annoyance by leaving you voice messages or e-mailing you repeatedly. In this, my final message to you, I would like to ask if you would like to speak with me now. I'm sitting at my desk right now and am prepared to speak with you. If this is not a good time, simply select "Reply" and propose an alternative date and time.

Regards,

[Your name]

We've taken two minimally effective approaches—telephone prospecting and e-mail—combined them, and added the additional component of synchronous use (just as you do when it is important that you reach someone) in order to obtain a better result.

Some things to remember:

- It is *essential* that these two methods be used together *synchronously.*
- You will find that when you attempt to *engage prospects at their time of need* (triggering event), it's even more effective.
- When voice mail and e-mail are used together, the *response rate increases.*
- The *messages* should point to a critical issue the prospect is dealing with.
- It's all about what the prospect is dealing with, *not what you are selling.*
- Your word choice, tone, organization, and pace are critical to the success of the process.
- Make it easy for prospects to engage, and *invite them to contact you immediately, while you are available.*
- Through this approach, prospects now have both a verbal and written record of your attempts to reach them and what it is that you wanted to speak with them about.

Checkpoint #21

_____ + _____ = thunder + lightning	
At what point is the thunder-and-lightning series most effective?	

Chapter 15

DIRECT MAIL PROSPECTING

Use of Direct Mail

This is a very underutilized approach. Once a primary method used by both salespeople and their marketing departments, direct mail is seldom used anymore. If you need convincing, just look at your own in-basket. There are nowhere near as many pieces as once were delivered. It's one of the reasons the U.S. postal service continues to evaluate curtailing services and closing offices. Direct mail has given way to e-mail and electronic delivery. As with other mediums of communication, direct mail has its own pros and cons.

Pros
- *The prospect is more receptive.* Unlike e-mail, where you are looking to see whom to "delete," when you review your postal mail, you're much more relaxed in attempting to determine what is important and what is not. A letter addressed to the recipient is looked upon more favorably and with interest.
- *It is becoming rarer and therefore special.* In this day of e-mail, most people don't use it.

- *You have the space and time you need.* You have the space and time to deliver a compelling message. If it is compelling, the recipient will stay with you, hold on to the correspondence, and share it.
- *You can include different pieces.* You have the ability to potentially capture the reader's interest by including a flyer, success story, color, etc.
- *Don't underestimate the ability to touch your brand.* Logo, letterhead, and color—it is who you are.

Cons

- *It is expensive.* Postage alone is very expensive.
- *It is time consuming.* Compiling address lists, addressing envelopes, printing the letters, stuffing the envelopes—that all takes time.
- *Delivery and response are a slow process.* It takes time for the mail to reach the recipient and time for the recipient to read it, and salespeople are not particularly patient. They want confirmation that the message has been received and read.
- *Prospects require multiple "touches" or mailers.* Typically it takes more than a single direct mail piece to gain any mindshare. The cost just continues to increase with every piece that is sent.

So why are we even discussing it? For all the reasons I listed under "Pros" above. The method of delivery, direct mail, adds to your uniqueness. It allows you to differentiate yourself from your competitors not only by the messages you are using, but also by the method you have chosen to deliver those messages. Your prospect, not used to receiving letters, may actually read it. You can simply use all the things we've discussed so far in this book and deliver the message differently. Consider taking a three–e-mail series that you have already carefully developed and turning it into a small, targeted direct mail campaign. Don't forget to monitor and track its effectiveness.

Checkpoint #22

Why can direct mail be a special method for you to reach your prospects?	
How is your prospect more receptive when receiving your direct mail piece?	

Chapter *16*

REFERRAL PROSPECTING

Importance of Referrals and How to Obtain Them

As we learned earlier, the number one reason that senior executives will choose to engage with a salesperson is a referral from inside or outside the company *(Source:* "Selling to Senior Executives," Kenan-Flagler Business School, University of North Carolina). Knowing this, who do you think might provide good referrals?

Satisfied Clients Are an Untapped Asset

Existing satisfied customers potentially represent a huge untapped asset for salespeople. Happy, satisfied customers will often brag about their selection, and as a result, they are more than happy to help a salesperson succeed with finding new accounts.

How to Ask for Referrals

The notion of asking an existing customer for a referral has been in sales books and courses forever. However, it has been my experience that salespeople fail to ask their customers—or if they do, they don't proactively manage the referrals they receive.

I think there are basically two types of referrals. I call them *general* and *targeted*.

General Referrals	Targeted Referrals
"Do you know of anyone who may be experiencing similar difficulties that you could refer or introduce me to?	"I see where you are a colleague of Sara Bell. Could you provide me with an introduction? I would be happy to draft something that you can sign and then send to her."

Other Referral Prospecting Methods

Here are other suggestions for good sources of referrals:

Social Network Contacts

- Comb your social network for individuals who may be able to provide you with a referral or introduction, and then use the "Get Introduced Through a Connection" capability on LinkedIn.

Build and Nurture a Referral Base

- If you are going to ask people for referrals and introductions, give them a reason for doing it. Give them a reason to say something good!

Utilize Available Technology

- Take advantage of the sales and referral tools that are available to you, e.g., InsideView, LinkedIn, etc.

Example of Asking for a Referral

From: Gary Walker
Sent: Tuesday, March 19, 2012, 8:26 a.m.
To: JSmith@firstsoftware.com
Cc: Kevin Kiernan
Subject: Referral from Kevin Kiernan

Dear Jim:

Our mutual colleague, Kevin Kiernan, referred me to you. I helped Kevin address the sales performance issues that he inherited when he was appointed Vice President of Sales at

Knowlagent. I have attached a success story that recaps what we were able to help him accomplish.

The top three complaints that I have been hearing from newly appointed senior sales executives are:

1. "The company has no defined sales process. The salespeople want to do their own thing."
2. "Too many good sales opportunities are being lost to 'no decision.'"
3. "Selling to these reps means discounting until the prospect says yes."

Did you inherit similar performance issues that you are going to need to address? If so, simply select "Reply," and we can schedule a mutually agreeable time to speak on the telephone.

Best,

Gary Walker
CustomerCentric Selling

Attachment: Knowlagent success story

Checkpoint #23

What are the two types of referrals you should ask for?

1.

2.

Chapter 17

DRIP MARKETING

What Is "Drip Marketing"?

Drip marketing is a direct marketing strategy that involves sending out several informational pieces over a period of time, at a set schedule, to those individuals you believe you need to speak with to get your offering sold, funded, and implemented.

Why Drip Marketing Is Important and How to Use It

Drip marketing will help you:

- Continue to communicate with people *who did not engage* with you
- Automatically *follow up* with new leads and people you have met
- Develop deeper *relationships* with new and old prospects
- *Automatically* elicit testimonials and case studies
- *Up-sell* and *cross-sell* existing customers automatically
- Automatically and consistently develop *quality referrals* from satisfied customers

Who Is Responsible for Drip Marketing?

For the most part, the answer to this question depends on the size of your company.

- *Large organizations.* Most large organizations have a centralized marketing function to whom you can hand off your prospects for further nurturing; drip marketing is part of a marketing department's strategy via e-newsletters, webinars, podcasts, etc. You want to take advantage of the professionally developed and branded communication pieces that the marketing department periodically distributes. Don't forget to augment marketing's efforts by communicating periodically with the people you have identified and would like to ultimately sell to.
- *Small organizations.* If you work for a small organization, in many cases it's up to you or it just doesn't happen. You will need to plan what it is that you are going to do, and with what frequency, taking advantage of any appropriate and professionally developed marketing pieces that might exist and utilizing some form of technology to communicate on a regular basis.

The Need for an Automated Delivery System

You will need some type of automated delivery system that you can use to develop, deliver, and monitor the success of your content and messaging. You may find that your company's SFA provides that capability, or you can utilize service providers such as ConstantContact (http://www.constantcontact.com). Once the system is developed and launched, the content will be delivered automatically.

Law of 29

There is a belief among many marketing professionals that an average prospect will not turn into a client until he or she has viewed the seller's marketing message at least 29 times. While I do not know that to be a proven statistical fact, I do know from my own experience that I need to stay in touch with my current and prospective clients in order for them to engage with me. There are way too many competitors out there not to.

Remaining Part of the Conversation

Salespeople give up too easily, and so they don't engage. Use drip marketing to remain in front of your clients and prospects by nurturing them with engaging and relevant information. The key is remaining part of the ongoing conversation with your prospects; drip nurturing can help you keep those lines of communication and access open.

Periodic Communication

Whether you have connected with the prospects or not, you are going to want to communicate with them on a regular basis to stay in front of them should needs change. This could mean up-selling a current client or cross-selling or selling into a new client based on your audience. You have placed your prospects in your database, and they are now part of your drip campaign. This can be completely automated with not a lot of effort on your part.

Engaging Content That Is Not Trying to Sell

The content should be aimed at educating and informing your prospects about topics that you know should be of interest to them. You are trying to establish your competency, be viewed as a resource of useful information, and be considered knowledgeable about each prospect's job and job issues.

Blogs and Discussions

Go where your prospects are going and interact with them by contributing to topics relevant to them. This will exhibit your thought leadership and expertise in that area, lending more to your credibility and exposure to the prospects.

Relevant Content

If something happens within your marketplace that is not part of your planned drip campaign, don't be afraid to change your planned message—utilize whatever is topical, relevant, and newsworthy. Keep in mind the problems or challenges that your prospects might be experiencing so that you can find and feed content relevant to them that sets up you and your company's offering at the point of need.

Articles and News of Interest

The content doesn't have to be original to you. If you find news or articles worth sharing, share them, especially if the information is relevant to your audience and relates to something of interest to your prospects.

Newsletters

If your company publishes an e-newsletter, put your prospects on the distribution list. They can always opt out if they don't find the newsletter beneficial or helpful. Newsletters and other regular communications are excellent ways to keep you and your company in front of your prospects as reminders that you're there to help, should their needs change from latent to active at any time.

Success Stories

Let prospective clients know whom you have helped and how you have helped them. It establishes you and your employer's competency while making it easier for them to admit a similar difficulty and request assistance. The key here is to remember that the best form of marketing is the voice of your own customers. Letting your customers tell their story comes across far more powerfully than hearing it from you.

Periodic Requests to Engage

From time to time, give prospects the opportunity to engage through a call or e-mail. You should be standing by the phone ready to help.

Getting Started with Drip Marketing

Here are some tips on how to get started with drip marketing:
- Identify the companies you would like to do business with:
  - Use InsideView to research the company—key executives, issues, press releases, etc.

- Identify the job titles—remember, *sell, fund, and implement.*
- Develop a *provocative message* that aligns with your research.
- Identify who in your *LinkedIn database* knows the executive you are trying to reach. *Request a referral or an introduction.*
  - Make it easy for the person to recommend you.

When you get a referral, carefully craft your message to the prospect:

- Your message should point to an issue the prospect has and how you have helped.
- Include a call to action.
- *Follow up the referral or introduction* with . . .
  - A telephone call immediately followed by an e-mail—think *thunder and lightning!*
  - A written follow-up plan.
  - A telephone call that references the introduction and issue.
  - A letter or a LinkedIn InMail that references the introduction and issue.
- Use *multiple approaches* to reach the person.
- *Remain part of the conversation—drip, drip,* and *nurture* the relationship.

Checkpoint #24

What are eight ways you can remain part of the conversation?

1.

2.

3.

4.

5.

6.

7.

8.

Chapter *18*

GETTING STARTED

We've covered a lot of ground in the preceding pages. In addition to talking about the prospecting methods themselves, we introduced new and overlooked variables such as:

- Utilizing technologies to increase your productivity and do some of your research for you
- Combining minimally effective methods and using them together to increase their overall effectiveness
- Varying the order in which the combined methods are used
- Varying the frequency and timing of your messages to your prospects
- Using provocative messaging to grab the attention of your prospects and to differentiate you and your message from those of your competitors
- Utilizing triggering events to contact your prospects during their time of need

Who knew that there were so many little things that you could do to become more effective and obtain more satisfactory results?

Six "To-Dos" Before Developing Your Prospecting Plan

Now is the time to take everything we have introduced and suggested you do, along with those things you have created, and begin to put them into *action*. However, before you plow headlong into developing your prospecting plan, I'd like to suggest the following:

1. *Plan your campaign.* We discussed the importance of planning in Chapter 4. Before you do anything else, plan what it is that you are going to do. You want it to be professional and impactful.
2. *Prepare.* Are you prepared? Gather up and organize the companies, individuals, contact information, messaging, methods, timetable, etc.
3. *Identify and use triggering events.* Are you going to seize upon a triggering event(s) to engage with your prospects? Will it be a targeted triggering event (example: newly hired or promoted) or a group triggering event (example: recent legislation that could affect a large group of potential prospects) that could require them to change how they do business today?
4. *Develop and use a menu of goals.* Will you be building your campaign around goals, problems, or needs? Are they what are keeping your prospects up at night? Is it about them, not you?
5. *Use a multiple-method approach.* What methods will you employ and in what order? The success of the methods can be enhanced when using them in cooperation with another; think *thunder and lightning*.
6. *Nurture and cultivate your prospects using a drip campaign.* If the prospects don't initially engage, are you prepared to place them into a drip marketing campaign in an attempt to gain mindshare and establish yourself as their go-to resource?

Execute a "25-Company Prospecting Plan"

I have found that despite everything we have introduced and explained in this book, some salespeople simply don't know how to plan. The idea of creating a plan is too difficult for some people to wrap their head around. If you're one of those people, and even if you're not,

I have created a *25-Company Prospecting Plan* (see next page) that you can use to get started.

It begins with planning, is followed by preparation, and then proceeds to daily actionable steps. In developing this plan, I have attempted to make it as granular as possible without making it too tedious. However, remember, it is *work*! Additionally, I have tried to be sensitive to a salesperson's time. However, in doing so, this plan does assume that you have set aside a minimum of two hours of valuable time every day, as suggested, dedicated to prospecting and business development.

Could this plan be expanded to include more companies? Sure it could. But if you make it too large, it may become unmanageable. If it becomes unmanageable, you'll neglect it for other things that require your attention, and the next thing you know, you are back to where you started—trying to figure out what you can do to increase the size and quality of your sales pipeline.

25-Company Prospecting Plan

Day	Action Step	Frequency	Individual or Group	Time Required	Completed (Yes or No)
	Step 1. *Build a list of companies* List a minimum of 25 companies. If you have it, use InsideView and its filtering capabilities to identify those companies that meet your marketing and sales criteria. If you don't have InsideView, sign up for a free limited-use version on the company's website: http://www.insideview.com.	As needed	Individual	30 minutes	
	Step 2. *Determine Key Players* For each of the companies you identified in step 1, determine a minimum of three Key Players per company. These are the people who can *buy, fund, and implement* your offering. *Remember:* You can't sell to someone who can't buy.	As needed	Individual or group	30 minutes	
	Step 3. *Develop a menu of goals* Discuss and agree upon a menu of goals—*high-probability business issues*—that the Key Players you identified in step 2 are faced with or are trying to achieve. *Remember:* Goals are typically the inverse of problems or needs. For example: Goal = achieve revenue goals. Problem or need = not meeting revenue goals.	As needed	Individual or group	30 minutes	

Step 4. *Identify triggering events* What types of activities do you believe could potentially *create an opportunity for you and your offering*—a change in leadership, a merger, regulatory changes, missed projections, something else?	Periodically revisit and refresh	Individual or group	30 minutes
Step 5. *Begin monitoring triggering events* Use your existing monitoring capabilities and also sign up for a free trial of InsideView, as well as any other methods you have available to you, to begin monitoring the companies you identified in step 1 for the *triggering events* you identified in step 4. You can create custom search agents in InsideView or use the standard search agents.	Daily	Individual	Automatic
Step 6. *Set up alerts* Go to your "watch list," the list of companies that you developed in step 1 and that is now your InsideView watch list. Select "Alerts" (envelope icon) at the top right-hand side of the page and specify how often you would like to be alerted to the triggering events you specified in step 4. With the completion of this step, you should begin receiving a daily e-mail containing triggering-event information about the companies.	Periodically	Individual or group	Automatic

Continued on next page

Day	Action Step	Frequency	Individual or Group	Time Required	Completed (Yes or No)
	Step 7. *Develop the thunder-and-lightning script series* Thunder and lightning is the method you are using to deliver your prospecting messages and scripts. The scripts have to be compelling and interesting. If they are not, they won't work. *Think provocative!* *People place three times more emphasis on loss than they do on gain.* Using the script examples and templates I introduced in this field guide, develop a series of three voice mails and e-mails. Collaborate with colleagues and share; review the material; read the e-mails and scripts out loud to each other; select what you feel are the most pointed, provocative, and interesting. Save these scripts and e-mails in Salesforce.com or MS Dynamics so that they will always be available to you.	As needed	Group	1 to 2 hours	
	Step 8. *Set aside sacred prospecting time* This is your uninterrupted time each day when you are going to do nothing but *prospect!* You don't take inbound calls. You don't check or respond to e-mails. You just prospect.	Daily	Individual	2 to 3 hours	

		Daily	Individual	2 to 3 hours	
	Step 9. Make it manageable Plan your activity and make it work. Don't make it so overwhelming that you are unable to continue. Let's start with five companies per day.				
Day 1	Contact the first group of five companies on your list. Make 15 outbound calls and send corresponding e-mails using script and e-mail series #1. 3 Key Players = 15 outbound thunder-and-lightning messages	Daily	Individual	2 to 3 hours	
Day 2	Contact the second group of five companies on your list. Make 15 outbound calls and send corresponding e-mails using script and e-mail series #1.	Daily	Individual	2 to 3 hours	

Continued on next page

Day	Action Step	Frequency	Individual or Group	Time Required	Completed (Yes or No)
Day 3	Contact the third group of five companies on your list. Make 15 outbound calls and send corresponding e-mails using script and e-mail series #1. Contact the first group of five companies on your list for the second time. Make 15 outbound calls and send corresponding e-mails using script and e-mail series #2.	Daily	Individual	2 to 3 hours	
Day 4	Contact the fourth group of five companies on your list. Make 15 outbound calls and send corresponding e-mails using script and e-mail series #1. Contact the second group of five companies on your list for the second time. Make 15 outbound calls and send corresponding e-mails using script and e-mail series #2.	Daily	Individual	2 to 3 hours	
Day 5	Contact the fifth and final group of five companies on your list. Make 15 outbound calls and send corresponding e-mails using script and e-mail series #1.	Daily	Individual	2 to 3 hours	

	Task	Frequency	Type	Time
	Contact the third group of five companies on your list for the second time. Make 15 outbound calls and send corresponding e-mails using script and e-mail series #2. Contact the first group of five companies on your list for the third time. Make 15 outbound calls and send corresponding e-mails using script and e-mail series #3.			
Day 6	Contact the second group of five companies on your list for the third time. Make 15 outbound calls and send corresponding e-mails using script and e-mail series #3. Contact the fourth group of five companies on your list for the second time. Make 15 outbound calls and send corresponding e-mails using script and e-mail series #2.	Daily	Individual	2 to 3 hours
Day 7	Place the first group of five into a drip marketing campaign. These are the companies and people that didn't engage whom you want to do business with through monthly contact at a minimum, e.g., through the company e-newsletter, etc.	Daily	Individual	2 to 3 hours

Once you have completed the above plan, it's time to begin returning calls and doing other sales-related work.

Counting "prep" time and execution time, it took you approximately 11 days to process 25 companies and potentially 75 individuals through a prospecting plan that included 225 phone calls (voice mails) and 225 e-mails, before placing individuals into a drip marketing campaign.

Checkpoint #25

Before you do anything in your prospecting efforts, you should first do what?	
You should be sure to use what in basing your initial contact with your prospects?	
What important tool will you use to organize your prospects' goals, problems, and needs?	
If, at first contact, your prospect does not wish to engage, what should you do?	
What combination of prospecting methods will give you higher hit rates?	

● ● ●

I hope that you have found this book to be helpful in discovering that prospecting and business development are more than cold calling and e-mail blasts. If you would like to participate in a one-day Prospecting and Business Development Workshop to expand on these concepts and sharpen your skills in an interactive and hands-on environment, please visit http://www.customercentric.com to find available workshop locations and dates and register online. Good selling!

Sources

About.com Marketing: http://marketing.about.com/cs/direct
    marketing/a/dripmktg.htm

A Case Study of Drip Campaigns: http://groundwire.org/resources/
    articles/dripcampaigns?searchterm=a+case+study+of+Drip

ConnectAndSell: http://www.connectandsell.com

ConstantContact: http://www.constantcontact.com

CustomerCentric Selling, Second Edition, by Michael T. Bosworth,
    John R. Holland, and Frank Visgatis

*Don't Cold Call. Social Call—Prospect with Sales 2.0 Tools and
Social Networks*

Drip Marketing, Inc.: http://www.dripmarketing.com

In a Downturn, Provoke Your Customers by Philip Lay, Todd
    Hewlin, and Geoffrey Moore: http://hbr.org/2009/03/in-a
    -downturn-provoke-your-customers/ar/1#

InsideView: http://www.insideview.com

The Law of 29—E-Mail Drip Marketing Myth or Reality: http://blog
    .delivra.com/index.php/2009/12/the-law-of-29-drip-marketing
    -myth-or-reality

Lead411: http://www.lead411.com

LeadFormix: http://www.leadformix.com

Nigel Edelshain, CEO, Sales 2.0 (LLC)

Phone Works: http://www.phoneworks.com

Prospecting 2.0: The Cold Call Is Dead Webinar: http://www.inside
    view.com/EVENTS/ARCHIVES/anneke-webinar-042009.html

Rethinking the Sales Cycle: How Superior Sellers Embrace the Buying Cycle to Achieve a Sustainable and Competitive Advantage by John R. Holland and Tim Young

Sales 2.0: http://www.sales2.com

Selling in a Downturn Economy—A Summary: http://www.slide share.net/stakano/selling-in-a-downturn-economy-a-summary -1090291

Using LinkedIn® by Patrice-Anne Rutledge: http://my.safaribooks online.com/book/web-applications-and-services/social-media/ 9780789745095

Index

About the Author

Gary A. Walker is one of the cofounders of CustomerCentric Systems, LLC. His ability to identify trends and changes in the sales environment has helped change the dynamic of interaction between sellers and buyers through the development of CustomerCentric Selling®. Walker's vision has helped propel CustomerCentric Systems to one of the preeminent providers of sales process training and consulting. He has worked with companies such as Altia, CCI Europe, Guidance Software, Knowlagent, L3 Commercial Security and Detections Systems, MapQuest, NewsGator, Recondo Technology, Reval, Rivet Software, and Vertafore to name just a few. He has personally trained thousands of salespeople in North America and Europe. A graduate of Bryant University in Smithfield, RI, Walker resides in Morrison, Colorado.

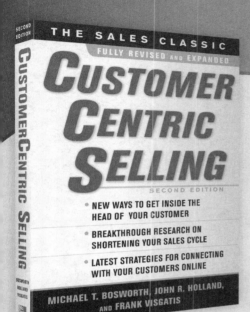